Officium Parbum B. V. M.

OFFICE

OF THE

Blessed Virgin Mary,

ACCORDING TO

THE USE OF THE CARMELITE ORDER.

Dolorosa Press
Camillus, New York

THE Little Office of the Blessed Virgin Mary of Mount Carmel, as contained in the following pages, is in perfect concordance with that contained in the Carmelite Breviary.

By authority,

MATTHEW SCALLY, o.c.c.

June 25, 1851.

Imprimatur:

Westmon. die 11 *Nov.* 1851,

N. CARD. WISEMAN.

To order additional copies, please contact:

Dolorosa Press
www.dolorosapress.com

Email: avemaria@dolorosapress.com

INDULGENCES

The faithful reciting the Little Office devoutly may gain an indulgence of 500 days for each hour recited, and an indulgence of 10 years for the recitation of the complete Office. Those reciting the entire Little Office before the Blessed Sacrament, either privately or chorally, may gain a plenary indulgence under the usual conditions.

The Psalms at Lauds follow the old arrangement prior to St. Pius X's 1911 revision of the Psalter which removed Psalms 66, 149, and 150. These three psalms are currently omitted in Little Office in virtue of the Apostolic Constitution Divino Afflatu of Saint Pius X. One may still use them, however, since this is a devotional office. One would thereby follow a most ancient tradition of the Church, namely the arrangement of Lauds already in use by the fifth century.

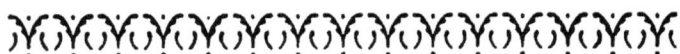

CARMELITE KALENDAR

JANUARY

2   St Euphrosyne, V.
16 St Peter Thomas, Bp, M.
19 St Telesphorus, Pope, M.
22 St Anastasius, M.
28 Bd Archangela, V.

FEBRUARY

4   St Andrew Corsini, Bp, Cf.
9   St Cyril, Bp of Alexandria, Cf, Doct.
25 St Avertanus, Cf.
    In Leap Years the feast of
    St Avertanus is kept on
    February 26th.

MARCH

3   Bd Jacobinus, Cf.
4   Bd Romaeus, Cf.
6   St Cyril of Constantinople, Bp, Cf.,
    Doct.
11 St Teresa Margaret Redi, V.
13 St Euphrasia, V.
20 Bd Baptist of Mantua, Cf.
29 St Berthold, Cf.
31 Bd Joan of Toulouse.

APRIL

18   Bd Mary of the Incarnation, Widow.

MAY

5   St Angelus, M.
11   Bd Aloysius Rabata, Cf.
16   St Simon Stock, Cf.
22   S. Joachima de Vedruna, Widow.
25   St Mary Magdalen de Pazzi, V.

JUNE

7   Bd Anne of St Bartholomew, V.
14   St Eliseus, Prophet, Father of our Order.

JULY

9   Bd Joan Scopelli, V.
16   Solemn Commemoration of Our Lady of Mount Carmel.
20   St Elias, Prophet, Father of our Order.
24   Bd Teresa of St Augustine and Companions, VV, MM.
26   St Anne, Mother of the BVM, Protectress of our Order.
28   Bd John Soreth, Cf.

AUGUST

7   St Albert of Sicily, Cf.
16   St. Joachim, Father of the BVM, Protector of our Order.
17   Bd Angelus Mazzinghi, Cf.
27   The Wounding of the Heart of St Teresa.

SEPTEMBER

2   St Brocard, Cf.
16   St Albert of Jerusalem, Cf., Lawgiver to our Order.
26   St Gerard, Bp, M.

OCTOBER

3   St Teresa of the Child Jesus, V.
15   St Teresa of Avila, V.
21   St Hilarion, Abbot.
30   St Serapion, Cf.

NOVEMBER

4   Bd Frances d'Amboise, Widow.
6   Bd Nonio, Cf.
14   All Saints of our Order.
15   Commemoration of all the faithful departed of our Order.
16   Bd Louis Morbioli, Cf.

24 St John of the Cross, Cf., Doct.
29 Bd Dionysius and Redemptus, MM.

DECEMBER

5 Bd Bartholomew Fanti, Cf.
11 Bd Francus, Cf.
14 St Spiridion, Bp, Cf.
16 Bd Mary of the Angels, V.
30 St Dionysius, Pope, Conf.

Abbreviations : Bp, Bishop; Cf, Confessor; Doct., Doctor of the Church; M, MM, Martyr, Martyrs; V, VV, Virgin, Virgins.

Rubrics

To be observed in the recitation of the Little Office of the Blessed Virgin

PUBLIC RECITATION

1. The public recitation of the Little Office presupposes the following officers for the choir: the Leader; two Cantors, one for each side of the choir; and two Versicularians, one for each side of the choir. Their functions are indicated in the following rubrics; and in the body of the Office the parts which they lead are indicated by the abbreviations proper to their titles (see page XII for the list of these abbreviations).

2. The choir is divided into two parts: the choir side, or side of the Leader; and the non-choir side. The Cantor on the choir side is called the First Cantor, and the one on the non-choir side is called the Second Cantor; the same distinction is made between the Versicularians.

3. The Leader, from his place, intones the opening and closing verses of all Hours, all antiphons; the verse *And lead us not* etc., the blessings, and the *Te Deum* in Matins; he

recites all chapters and prayers; he says the *Let us bless the Lord* in the little Hours and Compline; and the verse *May the souls* etc. at the end of all hours.

4. The two Cantors, standing in the middle of the choir, recite the Invitatory antiphon and psalm; intone all hymns, the first psalm of each Hour, all antiphons following psalms or canticles, the verse of the response to the third lesson of Matins, and the Canticles of Zachary, our Lady and Simeon.

5. Each Cantor, in his place, intones the psalms following the first psalm of each Hour when that psalm is to begin on his side of the choir. The First Cantor intones the responses to the first and third lessons of Matins, and the antiphons of all commemorations. The Second Cantor intones the response to the second lesson of Matins.

6. The two Versicularians, standing in the middle of the choir, recite all verses not said by the Leader; and the responses in the Little Hours. However, the verses of the comme morations and the *Blessed be the womb* etc. are recited by the First Versicularian in his place.

7. The lessons are read by the three youngest members of the choir, so that the youngest on the choir side reads the first lesson, the

youngest on the non-choir side the second, and the second youngest on the choir side the third. Before each lesson the reader, standing in the middle of the choir and facing the altar, bows and asks a blessing of the Leader. The verses of the responses to the first and second lessons are read by the second and third readers respectively.

8. All kneel for the Invitatory antiphon before and after the Invitatory psalm; at the words *Come, let us bow* etc. in the Invitatory psalm, for the verse *We beseech Thee* etc. in the *'Te Deum;'* for the first stanza of the hymn of Vespers.

9. All stand facing the middle of the choir for all hymns; the antiphons; the intonations of psalms; the *'Te Deum;'* the Canticles of Zachary, our Lady and Simeon; and the last psalm of Lauds.

10. The choir side sits for the second and fourth psalms; the non-choir side for the first, third and fifth psalms of all hours unless otherwise noted in the body of the Office. The side standing for the recitation of the psalms faces the middle of the choir. Both sides sit for the reading of the lessons and for their responses, until the *Glory be to the Father* etc. of the last response.

11. At other times all stand facing the altar.

12. All bow profoundly toward the middle of the choir as often as *Glory be to the Father* etc. is recited; for the verse *Let us bless the Father* etc. in the Canticle of the Three Youths; for the '*Our Father*' until *And lead us not* etc.; and for the prayer of the Office—not of commemorations—until the words *who is God, living* etc.

13. A profound bow is made at the name of Jesus, and at the words *Blessed be the name of the Lord;* a medium bow (slight inclination of head and shoulders) is made at the name of Mary; a slight bow (head only) is made at the names of commemorated saints.

14. If a Priest is the Leader, the Versicle and Response before the Prayer, are:

L.   The Lord be with you.

Comm.   And with thy spirit.

Preface

The Little Office of the Blessed Virgin is not merely a collection of prayers in honor of God's holy Mother. Like the Divine Office it is the official prayer of the Church in honor of Our Lady. All its wonders, efficacy and beauty are due to the fact that it enshrines so admirably what the inspired Scriptures, both indirectly and directly, proclaim of the power and dignity of her who is both Virgin and Mother. It teaches us what we ought to think about Our Lady, during each season of the year, how we ought to address her, and how best, through the prayers of the Little Office, to tell her of our needs. When we remember the constant use of the Little Office in the Church for so long a period and its recital by so many saints, any words of praise or appreciation seem presumptuous.

The Carmelite version of the Little Office, as might be expected, reflects the Marian spirituality of our Order, which was the first privileged to bear Our Lady's name. The use of the Marian Office is inculcated from novitiate days by means of choral recitation. For our Tertiaries the Office has the twofold advantage of amplifying the official praises of the Church and of the Order to which they belong. By means of it, they too will join in that official chorus that resounds unceasingly to glorify, to honor, to petition the Mediatrix of all graces and "the Hope of all Carmelites."

In this fifth centenary year of the founding of the Carmelite Third Order, it is most appropriate that in this new compilation the Office of our Tertiaries should once more make its most valuable contribution to the spiritual life of our Third Order members. It was to honor Our Lady that the Third Order was established by Blessed John Soreth, O. Carm., in 1452. He grieved, we are told, that among the laity there was no Order which officially constituted themselves Mary's children. When eventually the Third Order was instituted, the Little Office became its prayer book.

May this new compilation assist our Tertiaries in their efforts to realize that development of Marian life so well described by the Venerable Father Michael of St. Augustine, O. Carm., in his *Introductio ad Vitam Iternam*. There is summary he tells us:

The lofty stages of the Marian life are proper to Mary's singular lovers; and they are granted as special favors to those, her dearest children, whom she specially chooses. The Spirit of Jesus, Who produces in souls a filial love for the Eternal Father, then produces in them also filial affection and tender embraces and other acts of love for their dear Mother; and this He continues to do for all eternity. That Spirit, by Mary's co-operation, became her spirit, producing in her all forms of virtue and working all things in her and with her. When Mary deigns to fashion the souls of her favorite children, she procures for them her own spirit, which forms in them her virtues, her character, her mode of action, and her attractions. Thus it comes about that they seem to be identical with Mary, and the Spirit of Jesus dwells in them or, rather, lives and works in them; while they, as true children, become as one spirit with their amiable Mother, putting on the traits of her character. Their memory is occupied in the most simple manner with God and Mary; their intellect is occupied with a clear and pure knowledge of God's presence in it and of Mary in God; and their will is occupied with a most tranquil, deep, sweet, tender and spiritual love for God and for Mary in God, and with a loving adherence to God and to Mary in God.

PATRICK W. RUSSELL, O. CARM
Prior Provincial

Priory of Our Lady of the Scapular
Feast of the Patronage of Our Lady
January 30, 1953

APERI, Domine, os meum ad benedicendum nomen sanctum tuum. Munda quoque cor meum ab omnibus vanis, perversis, et alienis cogitationibus. Intellectum illumina, affectum inflamma; ut digne, attente, ac devote hoc Officium recitare valeam, et exaudiri merear ante conspectum divinæ Majestatis tuæ. Per Christum Dominum nostrum. Amen.

Domine, in unione illius divinæ intentionis, qua ipse in terris laudes Deo persolvisti, has tibi Horas persolvo.

Orationem sequentem devote post Officium recitantibus Leo Papa X. defectus et culpas in eo persolvendo, ex humana fragilitate contractas, indulsit.

SACROSANCTÆ et individuæ Trinitati, crucifixi Domini nostri Jesu Christi humanitati, beatissimæ et gloriosissimæ semperque Virginis Mariæ fœcundæ integritati, et omnium Sanctorum universitati, sit

Open thou my mouth, O Lord, to bless thy holy name: cleanse my heart also from all vain, perverse, and distracting thoughts; enlighten my understanding, inflame my affections, that I may recite this Office of the blessed Virgin Mary with worthy attention and devotion, and may deserve to be heard in the sight of thy divine Majesty; through Christ our Lord. Amen.

O Lord, I offer these hours unto thee, in union with that divine intention wherewith thou didst thyself offer praises to God whilst thou wast on earth.

To those who devoutly say the following prayer after Office, Leo X. granted an indulgence for any defects and faults in its recital arising from human frailty.

Everlasting praise, honour, power, and glory be given by all creatures to the most holy and undivided Trinity, to the humanity of our crucified Lord Christ Jesus, to the fruitful purity of the most blessed and most glorious Mary ever Virgin, sempiterna laus, honor, virtus, et gloria ab omni creatura, nobisque remissio omnium peccatorum, per infinita sæcula sæculorum. Amen.

℣. Beata viscera Mariæ Virginis, quæ portaverunt æterni Patris Filium.

℟. Et beata ubera, quæ lactaverunt Christum Dominum.

Pater noster. Ave Maria.

and to the company of all the saints; and may we obtain the remission of all our sins through all eternity. Amen.

℣. Blessed is the womb of the Virgin Mary, that bore the Son of the eternal Father.

℟. And blessed are the paps that gave suck to Christ our Lord.

Our Father. Hail Mary.

THE

Office of the Blessed Virgin Mary,

USE OF THE CARMELITE ORDER.

———◆———

AD MATUTINUM.

Ave Maria, *secreto, quæ dicitur semper in principio omnium Horarum B.M.V.*

AVE María, grátia plena, Dóminus tecum : benedícta tu in muliéribus, et benedíctus fructus ventris tui Jesus. Sancta María, Mater Dei, ora pro nobis peccatóribus, nunc, et in hora mortis nostræ. Amen.

℣. Dómine, labia mea apéries.

℟. Et os meum annuntiábit laudem tuam.

℣. Deus, in adjutórium meum inténde.

℟. Dómine, ad adjuvándum me festína.

℣. Glória Patri, et Fílio, et Spirítui Sancto.

℟. Sicut erat in princípio, et nunc, et semper, et in sæcula sæculórum. Amen.

In fine Alleluia, *ad omnes Horas, per totum annum,*

MATINS.

Hail Mary, *secretly, which is always said at the beginning of all the hours of the B. V. M.*

HAIL Mary, full of grace, the Lord is with thee : blessed art thou among women, and blessed is the fruit of thy womb, Jesus. Holy Mary, mother of God, pray for us sinners, now and at the hour of our death. Amen.

℣. Thou shalt open my lips, O Lord.

℟. And my mouth shall shew forth thy praise.

℣. O God, stretch forth unto mine aid.

℟. O Lord, make haste to help me.

℣. Glory be to the Father, and to the Son, and to the Holy Ghost.

As it was in the beginning, is now, and ever shall be, world without end. Amen.

Alleluia *at all the hours, throughout the year, except from Sep-*

præterquam a Septuagesi-
ma usque ad Sabbatum
sanctum, cujus loco tunc
dicitur : Laus tibi, Domine, Rex æternæ gloriæ.

tuagesima to Holy Saturday,
when, instead of Alleluia, is
said : Praise be to thee, O
Lord, King of everlasting
glory.

Invitatorium.

AVE María, grátia plena,
Dóminus tecum. Re-
petitur. Ave Maria, &c.

Invitatory.

Hail Mary, full of grace, the
Lord is with thee. Repeated.
Hail Mary, &c.

PSALMUS XCIV.

VENITE, exultémus Dó-
mino, jubilémus Deo
salutári nostro: præoccupé-
mus fáciem ejus in confessióne, et in psalmis jubilémus ei.
Ave María, grátia plena,
Dóminus tecum.
Quóniam Deus magnus
Dóminus, et Rex magnus
super omnes Deos : quóni-
am non repéllet Dóminus
plebem suam, quia in manu
ejus sunt omnes fines terræ,
et altitúdines móntium ipse
cónspicit.
Dóminus tecum.
Quóniam ipsíus est mare,
et ipse fecit illud, et áridam
fundavérunt manus ejus.
Veníte, adorémus et proci-
dámus ante Deum; ploré-
mus coram Dómino, qui fecit
nos, quia ipse est Dóminus
Deus noster,nos autempópu-
lus ejus et oves páscuæ ejus.
Ave María, &c.

PSALM XCIV.

O come, let us sing unto the
Lord, let us rejoice before God
our Saviour: let us come into
his presence with thanksgiving,
and with psalms rejoice before
him.
Hail Mary, full of grace, the
Lord is with thee.
For the Lord is a great God,
and a great King above all gods :
the Lord will not cast off his
people; in his hands are all the
ends of the earth, and he be-
holdeth the heights of the mountains.
The Lord is with thee.
The sea is his, and he made
it, and his hands founded the
dry land : come, let us adore
and fall down before God ; let
us lament before the Lord who
made us ; for he is the Lord our
God : we are his people, and the
sheep of his pasture.
Hail Mary, &c.

Hódie si vocem ejus audiéritis, nolíte obduráre corda vestra, sicut in exacerbatióne secúndum diem tentatiónis in deserto, ubi tentavérunt me patres vestri, probavérunt me, et vidérunt ópera mea.

Dóminus tecum.

Quadragínta annis próximus fui generatióni huic, et dixi: Semper hi errant corde: Ipsi vero non cognovérunt vias meas, quibus jurávi in ira mea, si introíbunt in réquiem meam.

Ave María, grátia plena, Dóminus tecum.

Gloria Patri, &c.

Dóminus tecum.

Ave Maria, &c.

To-day if ye shall hear his voice, harden not your hearts, as in the provocation, and as in the day of temptation in the wilderness; where your fathers tempted me, proved, and saw my works.

The Lord is with thee.

Forty years long was I nigh unto this generation, and said: They do always err in their heart: for they have not known my ways: unto whom I sware in my wrath, that they should not enter into my rest.

Hail Mary, full of grace, the Lord is with thee.

Glory be to the Father, &c.

The Lord is with thee.

Hail Mary, &c.

HYMNUS.

QUEM terra, pontus, sídera
Colunt, adórant, prædicant,
Trinam regéntem máchinam
Claustrum Maríæ bájulat.

Cui luna, sol, et ómnia
Desérviunt per témpora,
Perfúsa cœli grátia,
Gestant puéllæ víscera.

Beáta Mater múnere
Cujus supérnus Artifex
Mundum pugíllo cóntinens,
Ventris sub arca clausus est.

HYMN.

The Lord, whom earth, and sea, and sky, [claim;
With one adoring voice pro-
Who rules them all in majesty;
Enclos'd himself in Mary's frame.

Lo! in a humble Virgin's womb,
O'ershadowed by Almighty power;
He whom the stars, and sun, and moon, [hour.
Each serve in their appointed

O Mother blest! to whom was given
Within thy body to contain
The Architect of earth and heaven, [tain.
Whose hands the universe sus-

Beáta cœli núntio,
Fœcúnda Sancto Spíritu;
Desiderátus Géntibus,
Cujus per alvum fusus est.

Jesu, tibi sit glória,
Qui natus es de Vírgine,
Cum Patre, et almo Spíritu,
In sempitérna sæcula.
Amen.

*Tres Psalmi sequentes dicun-
tur die Dominica, Feria* ii.
et v. *ad Nocturnum.*
Ant. Benedicta tu,

PSALMUS VIII.

DOMINE Dóminus nos-
ter, * quam admirábile
est nomen tuum in univérsa
terra!

Quóniam eleváta est mag-
nificéntia tua* super cœlos.

Ex ore infántium et lac-
téntium perfecísti laudem
propter inimícos tuos;* ut
déstruas inimícum et ultó-
rem.

Quóniam vidébo cœlos
tuos, ópera digitórum tuórum; * lunam et stellas,quæ
tu fundásti.

Quid est homo, quod me-
mor es ejus? * aut fílius hó-
minis,quóniam vísitas eum?

Minuísti eum paulo mi-
nus ab Angelis, glória et
honóre coronásti eum ;* et
constituísti eum super ópera
mánuum tuárum.

To thee was sent an angel down;
In thee the Spirit was en-
  shrin'd;   [one,
Of thee was born that mighty
The long-desir'd of all man-
  kind.
O Jesu! born of Virgin bright,
Immortal glory be to thee;
Praise to the Father infinite,
And Holy Ghost eternally.
Amen.

*The three following Psalms are
said on Sunday, Monday, and
Thursday, at the Nocturn.*
Ant. Blessed art thou.

PSALM VIII.

1 O Lord, our Lord: how wonderful is thy name in all the
earth!

2 For thy greatness is exalted:
above the heavens.

3 Out of the mouth of babes
and sucklings hast thou perfected praise, because of thine enemies: that thou mayest destroy
the enemy and the avenger.

4 For I will behold thy heavens, the works of thy fingers :
the moon and the stars, which
thou hast founded.

5 What is man, that thou art
mindful of him: or the son of
man, that thou visitest him?

6 Thou hast made him a little
lower than the Angels, thou hast
crowned him with glory and
honour : and hast set him over
the works of thy hands.

Omnia subjecísti sub pédibus ejus;* oves et boves univérsas, ínsuper et pécora campi.

Vólucres cœli, et pisces maris,* qui perámbulant sémitas maris.

Dómine Dóminus noster,* quam admirábile est nomen tuum in univérsa terra! Glória Patri.

7 Thou hast put all things in subjection under his feet : all sheep and oxen, yea and the beasts of the field.

8 The birds of the air, and the fishes of the sea : that walk through the paths of the sea.

9 O Lord, our Lord : how wonderful is thy name in all the earth !

Glory, &c.

PSALMUS XVIII.

CŒLI enárrant glóriam Dei;* et ópera mánuum ejus annúntiat firmaméntum.

Dies diéi erúctat verbum,* et nox nocti índicat sciéntiam.

Non sunt loquélæ neque sermónes,* quorum non audiántur voces eórum.

In omnem terram exívit sonus eórum;* et in fines orbis terræ verba eórum.

In sole pósuit tabernáculum suum;* et ipse tanquam sponsus procédens de thálamo suo :

Exultávit ut gigas ad curréndam viam;* a summo cœlo egréssio ejus :

Et occúrsus ejus usque ad summum ejus ;* nec est qui se abscóndat a calóre ejus.

Lex Dómini immaculáta,

PSALM XVIII.

1 The heavens declare the glory of God : and the firmament proclaimeth the works of his hands.

2 Day unto day uttereth speech : and night unto night sheweth knowledge.

3 There is neither tongue nor language : in which their voices are not heard.

4 Their sound is gone forth into all the earth : their words unto the ends of the world.

5 He hath set his tabernacle in the sun : and he cometh forth as a bridegroom from his chamber.

6 He hath rejoiced as a giant to run his course : his going forth is from the topmost part of the heaven.

7 And his circuit even unto the height thereof : neither is there any that can hide himself from his heat.

8 The law of the Lord is un-

convértens ánimas;* testimónium Dómini fidéle, sapiéntiam præstans párvulis.

Justítiæ Dómini rectæ, lætificántes corda;* præcéptum Dómini lúcidum, illúminans óculos.

Timor Dómini sanctus, pérmanens in sæculum sæculi;* judicia Dómini vera. justificáta in semetípsa.

Desiderabília super aurum et lápidem pretiósum multum;* et dulcióra super mel et favum.

Etenim servus tuus custódit ea;* in custodiéndis illis retribútio multa.

Delícta quis intélligit? Ab occúltis meis munda me;* et ab aliénis parce servo tuo.

Si mei non fúerint domináti, tunc immaculátus ero;* et emundábor a delícto máximo.

Et erunt ut compláceant elóquia oris mei;* et meditátio cordis mei in conspéctu tuo semper.

Dómine, adjútor meus:* et redémptor meus. Glória.

---

defiled, converting souls : the testimony of the Lord is faithful, giving wisdom unto little ones.

9 The statutes of the Lord are right, rejoicing the heart : the commandment of the Lord is clear, enlightening the eyes.

10 The fear of the Lord is holy, enduring for ever and ever: the judgments of the Lord are true, justified in themselves.

11 More to be desired are they than gold, and all precious stones : sweeter also than honey and the honeycomb.

12 For thy servant keepeth them : and in keeping them there is great reward.

13 Who understandeth sins? cleanse thou me from my secret faults : and from the sins of others spare thy servant.

14 If they have had no dominion over me, then shall I be undefiled : and shall be cleansed from the greatest sin.

15 And the words of my mouth shall be pleasing to thee : and the meditation of my heart shall be always in thy sight.

16 O Lord, my helper : and my redeemer. Glory, &c.

PSALMUS XXIII.

DOMINI est terra, et plenitúdo ejus;* orbis ter-

PSALM XXIII.

1 The earth is the Lord's, and the fulness thereof : the compass

rárum, et univérsi qui hábitant in eo.

Quia ipse super mária fundávit eum,* et super flúmina præparávit eum.

Quis ascéndet in montem Dómini?* aut quis stabit in loco sancto ejus?

Innocens mánibus et mundo corde,* qui non accépit in vano ánimam suam, nec jurávit in dolo próximo suo.

Hic accípiet benedictiónem a Dómino,* et misericórdiam a Deo salutári suo.

Hæc est generátio quæréntium eum,* quæréntium fáciem Dei Jacob.

Attóllite portas, príncipes, vestras, et elevámini portæ æternáles;* et introíbit Rex glóriæ.

Quis est iste Rex glóriæ? *Dóminus fortis et potens; Dóminus potens in prælio.

Attóllite portas, príncipes, vestras, et elevámini portæ æternáles;* et introíbit Rex glóriæ.

Quis est iste Rex glóriæ? * Dóminus virtútum ipse est Rex glóriæ. Glória.

Ant. Benedícta tu in muliéribus, et benedíctus fructus ventris tui.

℣. Sancta Dei Génitrix virgo semper María.

℟. Intercéde pro nobis

of the world, and all that dwell therein.

2 For he hath founded it upon the seas : and prepared it upon the floods.

3 Who shall ascend into the mountain of the Lord : or who shall stand in his holy place?

4 He that hath clean hands and a pure heart : that hath not taken his soul in vain, nor sworn deceitfully to his neighbour.

5 He shall receive blessing from the Lord : and mercy from God his Saviour.

6 This is the generation of them that seek him : of them that seek the face of the God of Jacob.

7 Lift up your gates, O ye princes, and be ye lift up, ye everlasting doors : and the King of glory shall come in.

8 Who is this King of glory? the Lord, strong and mighty; the Lord, mighty in battle.

9 Lift up your gates, O ye princes, and be ye lift up, ye everlasting doors : and the King of glory shall come in.

10 Who is this King of glory? the Lord of hosts, he is the King of glory. Glory.

Ant. Blessed art thou among women, and blessed is the fruit of thy womb.

℣. Holy Mother of God, Mary ever virgin.

℟. Intercede for us with the

ad Dóminum Deum nostrum.

Pater noster, *cum Lectionibus et reliquis, ut infra,* p. 19.

Tres Psalmi sequentes dicuntur Fer. iii. *et* vi. *ad Noct.*

Ant. Specie tua.

PSALMUS XLIV.

E RUCTAVIT cor meum verbum bonum :* dico ego ópera mea Regi.

Lingua mea cálamus scribæ,* velóciter scribéntis.

Speciósus forma præ fíliis hóminum, diffúsa est grátia in lábiis tuis :* proptérea benedíxit te Deus in ætérnum.

Accíngere gládio tuo super femur tuum,* potentíssime.

Spécie tua, et pulchritúdine tua;* inténde, próspere procéde, et regna.

Propter veritátem, et mansuetúdinem, et justítiam :* et dedúcet te mirabíliter déxtera tua.

Sagíttæ tuæ acútæ, pópuli sub te cadent, * in corda inimicórum Regis.

Sedes tua, Deus, in sæculum sæculi :* virga directiónis virga regni tui.

Dilexísti justítiam, et odísti iniquitátem :* proptérea unxit te Deus, Deus

Lord our God.

Our Father, *with the* Lessons, *&c. as at* p. 19.

The three following Psalms are said on Tuesday and Friday.

Ant. In thy comeliness.

PSALM XLIV.

1 My heart hath uttered a good word : I tell of my works unto the King.

2 My tongue is the pen of a scribe : that writeth very swiftly.

3 Thou art beautiful above the sons of men, grace is poured forth on thy lips : therefore hath God blessed thee for ever.

4 Gird thy sword upon thy thigh : O thou most mighty.

5 In thy comeliness and thy beauty : go forth, proceed prosperously, and reign.

6 Because of truth, and meekness, and justice : and thy right hand shall lead thee on wonderfully.

7 Thine arrows are sharp, and the people shall fall before thee : they shall pierce the hearts of the king's enemies.

8 Thy throne, O God, is for ever and ever : a sceptre of uprightness is the sceptre of thy kingdom.

9 Thou hast loved justice, and hated iniquity : therefore God, even thy God, hath anointed

tuus, óleo lætítiæ præ con-
sórtibus tuis.

Myrrha, et gutta, et cásia
a vestiméntis tuis, a dómi-
bus ebúrneis;* ex quibus
delectavérunttefíliæregum
in honóre tuo.

Astitit Regína a dextris
tuis in vestitu deauráto,*
circúmdata varietáte.

Audi fília, et vide, et in-
clína aurem tuam;* et obli-
víscere pópulum tuum, et
domum patris tui.

Et concupíscet Rex de-
córem tuum;* quóniam ipse
est Dóminus Deus tuus, et
adorábunt eum.

Et fíliæ Tyri in munéri-
bus,* vultum tuum depre-
cabúntur omnes dívites plebis.

Omnis glória ejus fíliæ
Regis ab intus,* in fímbriis
aureis circumamícta varie-
tátibus.

Adducéntur Regi vírgines
post eam;* próximæ ejus
afferéntur tíbi.

Afferéntur in lætítia et
exultatióne :* adducéntur
in templum Regis.

Pro.pátribus tuis nati sunt
tibi fílii :* constítues eos
príncipes super omnem terram.

Mémores erunt nóminis

thee with the oil of gladness
above thy fellows.

10 Myrrh, aloes, and cassia
perfume thy garments, from
the ivory palaces : whence the
daughters of kings have made
thee glad in thine honour.

11 Upon thy right hand stood
the queen in a vesture of gold :
wrought about with variety.

12 Hearken, O daughter, and
consider, and incline thine ear :
forget also thine own people,
and thy father's house.

13 And so shall the king desire thy beauty : for he is the
Lord thy God, and him shall
they adore.

14 And the daughters of Tyre,
with gifts : yea, all the rich
among the people shall entreat
thy countenance.

15 All the glory of the King's
daughter is from within : with
borders of gold, and clothed
about with varieties.

16 After her shall virgins be
brought unto the King : her companions shall be brought unto
thee.

17 With joy and gladness shall
they be brought : they shall be
led into the temple of the King.

18 Instead of thy fathers, sons
are born unto thee : thou shalt
make them princes over all the
earth.

19 They shall be mindful of

tui,* in omni generatióne et generatiónem.

Proptérea pópuli confitebúntur tibi in ætérnum,* et in sæculum sæculi. Glória.

thy name: from generation to generation.

20 Therefore shall the people praise thee for ever: yea, for ever and ever. Glory, &c.

PSALMUS XLV.

DEUS noster refúgium et virtus;* adjútor in tribulatiónibus, quæ invenérunt nos nimis.

Proptérea non timébimus, dum turbábitur terra,* et transferéntur montes in cor maris.

Sonuérunt et turbátæ sunt aquæ eórum;* conturbáti sunt montes in fortitúdine ejus.

Flúminis ímpetus lætíficat civitátem Dei:* sanctificávit tabernáculum suum Altíssimus.

Deus in médio ejus, non commovébitur;* adjuvábit eam Deus mane dilúculo.

Conturbátæ sunt Gentes, et inclináta sunt regna:* dedit vocem suam, mota est terra.

Dóminus virtútum nobíscum;*suscéptor noster Deus Jacob.

Veníte, et vidéte ópera Dómini, quæ pósuit prodígia super terram;* áúferens bella usque ad finem terræ.

Arcum cónteret, et con-

PSALM XLV.

1 Our God is a refuge and strength: our helper in troubles which have fallen on us heavily.

2 Therefore will we not fear when the earth shall be troubled: and the mountains shall be removed into the heart of the sea.

3 Their waters roared and were troubled: the mountains were troubled at the violence thereof.

4 The swelling of the stream maketh glad the city of God: the Most High hath sanctified his tabernacle.

5 God is in the midst of her, she shall not be moved: God shall help her in the morning early.

6 Nations were troubled, and kingdoms bowed down: he gave forth his voice, and the earth was moved.

7 The Lord of hosts is with us: the God of Jacob is our helper.

8 O come and behold the works of the Lord, what wonders he hath wrought upon the earth: making wars to cease, even unto the ends of the earth.

9 He shall break the bow, and

fringet arma ;* et acuta com·
búret igni.

Vacáte, et vidéte quóniam
ego sum Deus :* exaltábor
in Géntibus, et exaltábor in
terra.

Dóminus virtútum nobís-
cum :*suscéptor noster Deus
Jacob. Glória Patri.

PSALMUS LXXXVI.

FUNDAMENTA ejus in
móntibus sanctis :* di-
ligit Dóminus portas Sion,
super ómnia tabernácula
Jacob.

Gloriósa dicta sunt de te,*
cívitas Dei.

Memor ero Rahab et Ba-
bylónis,* sciéntium me.

Ecce alienígenæ, et Tyrus,
et pópulus Æthíopum,* hi
fuérunt illic.

Numquid Sion dicet: Ho-
mo, et homo natus est in ea ;
* et ipse fundávit eam Altíssimus?

Dóminus narrábit in scrip-
túris populórum et princi-
pum ;* horum, qui fuérunt
in ea.

Sicut lætántium omnium
* habitátio est in te.

Glória Patri.

Ant. Specie tua, et pulchritúdine tua, inténde, próspere
procéde, et regna.

℣. Post partum Virgo
invioláta permansísti.

knap the weapons in sunder:
and the shields shall he burn
with fire.

10 Be still, and see that I am
God: I will be exalted among
the nations, and I will be exalted in the earth.

11 The Lord of hosts is with
us: the God of Jacob is our
helper. Glory, &c.

PSALM LXXXVI.

1 Her foundations are upon
the holy hills: the Lord loveth
the gates of Sion more than all
the tabernacles of Jacob.

2 Glorious things are spoken
of thee : O thou city of God.

3 I will be mindful of Rahab
and Babylon: even of them that
know me.

4 Behold strangers, and Tyre,
and the people of Ethiopia: all
these were there.

5 Shall not Sion say, This
man and that were born in her :
and the Most High himself hath
founded her?

6 The Lord shall declare it in
the writings of people and of
princes : of all who were in her.

7 The dwelling in thee : is as
of all those that rejoice.

Glory, &c.

Ant. In thy comeliness and
thy beauty go forth, proceed
prosperously, and reign.

℣. After child-birth thou didst
remain a pure virgin.

℟. Dei Génitrix inter-
céde pro nobis.

Pater noster, *cum Lecti-*
onibus, &c. ut infra, p. 19.

Tres Psalmi sequentes di-
cuntur Feria iv. *et Sab-*
bato, ad Nocturnum.

Ant. Gaude, Maria Virgo.

℟. O Mother of God, intercede for us.

Our Father, *with the Lessons,*
&c. as at p. 19.

The three following Psalms are
said on Wednesday and Satur-
day.

Ant. Rejoice, O Virgin Mary.

PSALMUS XCV.

CANTATE Dómino cánti-
cum novum :* cantáte
Dómino omnis terra.

Cantáte Dómino, et bene-
dícite nómini ejus:* annuntiáte de die in diem salutáre
ejus.

Annuntiáte inter Gentes
glóriam ejus,* in ómnibus
pópulis mirabília ejus.

Quóniam magnus Dómi-
nus, et laudábilis nimis: *
terríbilis est super omnes
deos.

Quóniam omnes dii Gén-
tium dæmónia ;* Dóminus
autem cœlos fecit.

Conféssio et pulchritúdo
in conspéctu ejus ;* sancti-
mónia et magnificéntia, in
sanctificatióne ejus.

Afférte Dómino, pátriæ
Géntium, afférte Dómino
glóriam et honórem ;* afférte Dómino glóriam nómini
ejus.

Tóllite hóstias, et introíte
in átria ejus ;* adoráte Dóminum in átrio sancto ejus.

PSALM XCV.

1 Sing unto the Lord a new
song : sing unto the Lord, all
the earth.

2 Sing unto the Lord, and
bless his name : tell forth his
salvation from day to day.

3 Tell forth his glory among
the Gentiles : his wonders among
all people.

4 For the Lord is great, and
highly to be praised : he is more
to be feared than all gods.

5 For all the gods of the Gentiles are devils : but the Lord
made the heavens.

6 Praise and beauty are before
him : holiness and majesty in
his sanctuary.

7 Bring unto the Lord, O ye
kindred of the Gentiles, bring
unto the Lord glory and honour :
bring unto the Lord glory unto
his name.

8 Bring sacrifices, and come
into his courts : adore ye the
Lord in his holy court.

Commoveátur a fácie ejus univérsa terra :* dícite in Géntibus quia Dóminus regnávit.

Etenim corréxit orbem terræ, qui non commovébitur :* judicábit pópulos in æquitáte.

Læténtur cœli et exúltet terra, commoveátur mare, et plenitúdo ejus ;* gaudébunt campi, et ómnia quæ in eis sunt.

Tunc exultábunt ómnia ligna silvárum a fácie Dómini, quia venit ;* quóniam venit judicáre terram.

Judicábit orbem terræ in æquitáte,* et pópulos in veritáte sua.　Glória Patri.

PSALMUS XCVI.

DOMINUS regnávit, exúltet terra, * læténtur ínsulæ multæ.

Nubes et calígo in circúitu ejus ;* justítia, et judícium corréctio sedis ejus.

Ignis ante ipsum præcédet,* et inflammábit in circúitu inimícos ejus.

Illuxérunt fúlgura ejus orbi terræ :* vidit, et commóta est terra.

Montes sicut cera fluxérunt a fácie Dómini ;* a fácie Dómini omnis terra.

Annuntiavérunt cœli jus-

9 Let all the earth be moved at his presence : say ye among the Gentiles, that the Lord hath reigned.

10 For he hath established the world, and it shall not be moved : he shall judge the people with equity.

11 Let the heavens rejoice, and let the earth be glad ; let the sea be moved, and the fulness thereof : the fields shall be joyful, and all things that are therein.

12 Then shall all the trees of the wood rejoice before the face of the Lord, for he cometh : for he cometh to judge the earth.

13 He shall judge the world with equity : and the people with his truth.　Glory, &c.

PSALM XCVI.

1 The Lord hath reigned, let the earth rejoice : let the multitude of isles be glad thereof.

2 Clouds and darkness are round about him : justice and judgment are the foundation of his throne.

3 Fire shall go forth before him : and shall burn up his enemies on every side.

4 His lightnings shone upon the world : the earth saw, and was moved.

5 The mountains melted like wax before the face of the Lord : yea, all the earth before the face of the Lord.

6 The heavens declared his

títiam ejus ; * et vidérunt omnes pópuli glóriam ejus.

Confundántur omnes, qui adórant sculptília ;* et qui gloriántur in simulácris suis.

Adoráte eum, omnes Angeli ejus : * audívit, et lætáta est Sion.

Et exultavérunt fíliæ Judææ,* propter judícia tua Dómine :

Quóniam tu Dóminus Altissimus super omnem terram ;* nimis exaltátus es super omnes deos.

Qui dilígitis Dóminum, odíte malum ;* custódit Dóminus ánimas sanctórum suórum, de manu peccatóris liberábit eos.

Lux orta est justo,* et rectis corde lætítia.

Lætámini justi in Dómino,* et confitémini memóriæ sanctificatiónis ejus.

Glória Patri.

PSALMUS XCVII.

CANTATE Dómino cánticum novum,* quia mirabília fecit.

Salvávit sibi déxtera ejus, * et bráchium sanctum ejus.

Notum fecit Dóminus salutáre suum ;* in conspéctu Géntium revelávit justitiam suam.

Justice: and all people saw his glory.

7 Confounded be all they that adore graven things : and that glory in their idols.

8 Adore him, all ye his angels : Sion heard, and was glad.

9 And the daughters of Judah rejoiced : because of thy judgments, O Lord.

10 For thou, Lord, art most high over all the earth: thou art exalted exceedingly above all gods.

11 Ye who love the Lord, hate evil : the Lord preserveth the souls of his saints, he will deliver them out of the hand of the sinner.

12 Light is risen to the just : and gladness to such as are right of heart.

13 Rejoice in the Lord, O ye just : and give praise to the remembrance of his holiness.

Glory, &c.

PSALM XCVII.

1 Sing unto the Lord a new song : for he hath done wonderful things.

2 His right hand hath wrought salvation for him : and holy is his arm.

3 The Lord hath made known his salvation : he hath revealed his justice in the sight of the Gentiles.

Recordátus est misericór-
diæ suæ,* et veritátis suæ
dómui Israel.

Vidérunt omnes términi
terræ* salutáre Dei nostri.

Jubiláte Deo omnis terra;
* cantáte, et exultáte, et
psállite.

Psállite Dómino in cítha-
ra, in cíthara et voce psalmi ;
* in tubis ductílibus, et voce
tubæ córneæ.

Jubiláte in conspéctu Re-
gis Dómini : * moveátur
mare, et plenitúdo ejus; orbis
terrárum, et qui hábitant in
eo.

Flúmina plaudent manu,
simul montes exultábunt a
conspéctu Dómini;* quóni-
am venit judicáre terram.

Judicábit orbem terrárum
in justitia,* et pópulos in
æquitáte. Glória.

Ant. Gaude, María Virgo,
cunctas hæreses sola inter-
emísti in univérso mundo.

℣. Speciósa facta es et
suavis.

℟. In delíciis tuis, sancta
Dei Génitrix.

Pater noster (*secreto*).

℣. Et ne nos indúcas in
tentatiónem.

℟. Sed líbera nos a malo.

℣. Jube, domne, benedí-
cere.

4 He hath remembered his
mercy : and his truth towards
the house of Israel.

5 All the ends of the earth
have seen : the salvation of our
God.

6 Sing joyfully unto the Lord,
all ye lands : sing, and rejoice,
give praise.

7 Give praise unto the Lord
upon the harp, upon the harp,
and with the voice of psalms :
with the long trumpets and the
sound of the cornet.

8 Sing joyfully before the
Lord the King : let the sea be
moved, and the fulness thereof;
the compass of the earth, and
they that dwell therein.

9 The rivers shall clap their
hands, and the mountains shall
rejoice together at the presence
of the Lord: for he cometh to
judge the earth.

10 He shall judge the earth
with justice : and the people
with equity. Glory, &c.

Ant. Rejoice, O Virgin Mary,
thou alone hast destroyed all
heresies in the whole world.

℣. Thou art become beautiful
and sweet.

℟. In thy delights, O holy
Mother of God.

Our Father (*secretly*).

℣. And lead us not into temptation.

℟. But deliver us from evil.

℣. Pray, sir, a blessing.

Benedictio.

Alma Virgo vírginum intercédat pro nobis ad Dóminum. Amen.

LECTIO I. *Cant.* iii.

Q UÆ est ista, quæ ascéndit per desértum, sicut vírgula fumi ex aromátibus myrrhæ, et thuris, et univérsi púlveris pigmentárii? Tota pulchra es amíca mea, et mácula non est in te. Hortus conclúsus, soror mea sponsa, hortus conclúsus, fons signátus. Tu autem, Dómine, miserére nostri.

℞. Deo grátias.

℞. Sancta et immaculáta virgínitas, quibus te laudibus éfferam, néscio. * Quia quem cœli cápere non póterant, tuo grémio contulísti.[1]

℣. Benedícta tu in muliéribus, et benedíctus fructus ventris tui. * Quia quem.

℣. Jube, domne, benedícere.

Benedictio.

Nos cum prole pia benedicat Virgo María. ℞. Amen.

LECTIO II. *Ecclus.* xxiv.

E GO quasi terebinthus exténdi ramos meos, et rami mei honóris et grátiæ. Ego quasi vitis fruc-

The Blessing.

May gracious Virgin Mary intercede for us with the Lord. Amen.

LESSON I. *Cant.* iii. 6.

Who is she that goeth up by the desert, as a pillar of smoke of aromatical spices, of myrrh, and frankincense, and of all the powders of the perfumers? Thou art all fair, O my love, and there is not a spot in thee. My sister, my spouse, is a garden enclosed, a garden enclosed, a fountain sealed up. But thou, O Lord, have mercy on us.

℞. Thanks be to God.

℞. O holy and immaculate virginity, with what praises I shall extol thee, I know not : * For he whom the heavens could not contain rested in thy bosom.[1]

℣. Blessed art thou among women, and blessed is the fruit of thy womb. * For he whom, &c.

℣. Pray, sir, a blessing.

The Blessing.

May the Virgin Mary bless us with her loving Son.

LESSON II. *Ecclus.* xxiv. 22.

I have stretched out my branches as the turpentine-tree, and my branches are of honour and of grace. As the vine I

[1] In Easter-time *Alleluia* is added after the R. in each Lesson.

tificávi suavitátem odóris: et flores mei fructus honóris et honestátis. Ego mater pulchræ dilectiónis, et timóris, et agnitiónis, et sanctæ spei. In me grátia omnis viæ, et veritátis: in me omnis spes vitæ, et virtútis. Tu autem, Dómine, miserére nostri.

℞. Deo grátias.

℞. Beáta es, Virgo María, quæ Dóminum portásti Creatórem mundi. * Genuísti qui te fecit, et in ætérnum pérmanes virgo.

℣. Ave María, grátia plena, Dóminus tecum. * Genuísti.

℣. Jube, domne, benedícere.

Benedictio.

Sancta Dei Génitrix sit nobis auxiliátrix.

℞. Amen.

LECTIO III.

TRANSITE ad me omnes, qui concupíscitis me, et à generatiónibus meis implémini. Spíritus enim meus super mel dulcis, et hæréditas mea super mel, et favum. Memória mea in generatiónes sæculórum. Qui audit me, non confundétur: et qui operántur in me, non peccábunt. Qui elúcidant me, vitam ætérnam habébunt. Tu autem, Domine.

have brought forth a pleasant odour; and my flowers are the fruit of honour and riches. I am the mother of fair love, and of fear, and of knowledge, and of holy hope. In me is all grace of the way and of the truth; in me is all hope of life and of virtue. But thou, O Lord, have mercy on us.

℞. Thanks be to God.

℞. Blessed art thou, O Virgin Mary, who didst bear the Lord, the Creator of the world:* Thou wast the mother of him who made thee, and thou remainest a virgin for ever.

℣. Hail Mary, full of grace, the Lord is with thee. * Thou wast the mother, &c.

℣. Pray, sir, a blessing.

The Blessing.

May the holy Mother of God be our helper.

℞. Amen.

LESSON III. *Ecclus.* xxiv. 26.

Come over to me, all you who desire me, and you shall be filled from my fruits. For my spirit is sweet above honey, and my inheritance above honey and the honeycomb. My memory is unto everlasting generations. He that hearkeneth to me shall not be confounded; and they that work by me shall not sin. They that explain me shall have life everlasting. But thou, O Lord, have mercy on us.

℟. Deo grátias.

℟. Felix namque es, sacra Virgo María, et omni laude digníssima. * Quia ex te ortus est sol justítiæ, Christus Deus noster.

℣. Ora pro pópulo, intérveni pro clero, intercéde pro devóto fœmíneo sexu : séntiant omnes tuum juvámen, quicúmque célebrant tuam sanctam commemoratiónem. * Quia ex te.

Glória Patri, et Fílio, et Spirítui Sancto. Quia ex te. Christus Deus noster.

Quando in Officio diei a Nativitate usque ad Septuagesimam, et a Pascha usque ad Adventum, dicitur Te Deum, *dicitur etiam in Officio parvo : et quando in Officio diei non dicitur, nec in parvo Officio dicitur. In Adventu vero et a Septuagesima usque ad Pascha, non dicitur* Te Deum *in Officio parvo, etiam si in Officio diei dicatur.*

Ab iis autem, qui ex devotione illud recitant, in eo dicitur Te Deum *in diebus Conceptionis, Expectationis Partus (ubi recitatur ejus Officium), et Purificationis B. V. si de iisdem Festis recitatur Officium; alias in diebus,*

℟. Thanks be to God.

℟. Surely thou art happy, O holy Virgin Mary, and most worthy of all praise : * For out of thee arose the sun of justice,* Christ our God.

℣. Pray for the people, mediate for the clergy, intercede for the devoted female sex. Let all experience thy assistance, whoever celebrate thy holy commemoration. For out of thee, &c.

℣. Glory be to the Father, and to the Son, and to the Holy Ghost. For, &c. Christ our God.

When in the Office of the day from the Nativity to Septuagesima, and from Easter to Advent, the Te Deum *is said, it is also said in this Office; and when it is not said in the Office of the day, neither is it said here. But in Advent, and from Septuagesima Sunday to Easter,* Te Deum *is not said, even though it be said in the Divine Office of the day.*

By those, however, who recite the little Office solely out of devotion, whether clerical or lay, the Te Deum *is said on the Feasts of the Immaculate Conception, the Expectation of the B. V., and on the Feast of the Purification, if the Office of those Feasts be recited; other-*

*ad quos talia Festa trans-
feruntur.*
Dum vero Te Deum *non dicitur,* R̹. Felix, *propter
hoc non resumatur. Sa-
cerdotalis.*

R̹. Ora pro nobis sancta
Dei Génitrix.

R̹. Ut digni efficiámur
promissiónibus Christi.

*Hymnus SS. Ambrosii et
Augustini.*

TE Deum laudámus : * te
Dóminum confitémur.
Te ætérnum Patrem * om-
nis terra venerátur.
Tibi omnes Angeli, * tibi
Cœli, et univérsæ Potes-
tátes,
Tibi Chérubim et Séra-
phim, * incessábili voce pro-
clámant :
Sanctus, sanctus, sanc-
tus, * Dóminus Deus Sá-
baoth ;
Pleni sunt cœli et terra, *
majestátis glóriæ tuæ.
Te gloriósus * Apostoló-
rum chorus.
Te Prophetárum * laudá-
bilis númerus.
Te Mártyrum candidátus
* laudat exércitus.
Te per orbem terrárum *
sancta confitétur Ecclésia.

*wise on the days to which they
are transferred.*
When Te Deum *is not said, then
the* R̹. Thou art truly happy,
&c., *to the* V̹., *is said after the
third repetition of* Because out
of thee, &c.

V̹. Pray for us, O holy Mother
of God.

R̹. That we may be made worthy of the promises of Christ.

*Hymn of St. Ambrose and St.
Augustin.*

We praise thee, O God : we
acknowledge thee to be the Lord.
All the earth doth worship
thee : the Father everlasting.
To thee all angels cry aloud :
the heavens and all the powers
therein :
To thee cherubim and sera-
phim : continually do cry ;

Holy, holy, holy : Lord God of
Sabaoth.

Heaven and earth are full : of
the majesty of thy glory.
The glorious choir of the
Apostles : praise thee.
The admirable company of the
Prophets : praise thee.
The white-robed army of
Martyrs : praise thee.
The Holy Church throughout
all the world : doth acknowledge
thee.

Patrem* imménsæ majestátis.

Venerándum tuum verum *et únicum Fílium.

Sanctum quoque * Paráclitum Spíritum.

Tu Rex glóriæ,* Christe.

Tu Patris*sempitérnus es Fílius.

Tu ad liberándum susceptúrus hóminem,* non horruísti Vírginis úterum.

Tu devícto mortis acúleo, * aperuísti credéntibus regna cœlórum.

Tu ad déxteram Dei sedes, * in glória Patris.

Judex créderis* esse ventúrus.

Te ergo quæsumus, tuis fámulis súbveni,* quos pretióso sánguine redemísti.

Ætérna fac cum Sanctis tuis,* in glória numerári.

Salvum fac pópulum tuum, Domine,* et bénedic hæreditáti tuæ.

Et rege eos, et extólle illos,* usque in ætérnum.

Per síngulos dies* benedícimus te.

Et laudámus nomen tuum in sæculum,* et in sæculum sæculi.

Dignáre, Dómine, die is-

The Father : of an infinite majesty.

Thy adorable, true : and only Son.

Also the Holy Ghost : the Comforter.

Thou art the King of Glory : O Christ.

Thou art the everlasting Son : of the Father.

When thou tookest upon thee to deliver man : thou didst not abhor the Virgin's womb.

When thou hadst overcome the sting of death : thou didst open the kingdom of heaven to all believers.

Thou sittest at the right hand of God : in the glory of the Father.

We believe that thou shalt come : to be our Judge.

We pray thee, therefore, help thy servants : whom thou hast redeemed with thy precious blood.

Make them to be numbered with thy Saints : in glory everlasting.

O Lord, save thy people : and bless thine inheritance.

Govern them : and lift them up for ever.

Day by day: we magnify thee.

And we praise thy name for ever : yea, for ever and ever.

Vouchsafe, O Lord, this day :

to,* sine peccáto nos custo-
díre.

Miserére nostri, Dómine,*
miserére nostri.

Fiat misericórdia tua, Dómine, super nos :* quemád-
modum sperávimus in te.

In te, Dómine, sperávi;*
non confúndar in ætérnum.

Sacerdotalis.

℣. Ora pro nobis sancta
Dei Génitrix.

℟. Ut digni efficiámur
promissiónibus Christi.

AD LAUDES.

Ave Maria.

DEUS, in adjutórium me-
um inténde.

℟. Domine, ad adjuván-
dum me festína.

℣. Glória Patri.

℟. Sicut erat. Alleluia.

Ant. Assumpta est.

PSALMUS XCII.

DOMINUS regnávit, decó-
rem indútus est :* in-
dútus est Dóminus fortitú-
dinem, et præcínxit se.

Etenim firmávit orbem
terræ,* qui non commové-
bitur.

Paráta sedes tua ex tunc :*
a sæculo tu es.

Elevavérunt flúmina, Dó-

to keep us without sin.

O Lord, have mercy upon us :
have mercy upon us.

O Lord, let thy mercy be
shewed upon us : as we have
hoped in thee.

O Lord, in thee have I hoped :
let me not be confounded for
ever.

℣. Pray for us, O holy Mother
of God.

℟. That we may be made
worthy of the promises of Christ.

AT LAUDS.

Hail Mary.

℣. O God, stretch forth unto
mine aid.

℟. O Lord, make haste to
help me.

Glory, &c.

As it was, &c.   Alleluia.

Ant. Mary was taken up.

PSALM XCII.

1 The Lord hath reigned, he
is clothed with beauty : the Lord
is clothed with strength, and
hath girded himself therewith.

2 For he hath established the
world : and it shall not be
moved.

3 Thy throne is prepared of
old : thou art from everlasting.

4 The floods have lifted up

mine,* elevavérunt fiúmina vocem suam.

Elevavérunt fiúmina fluctus suos,* a vócibus aquárum multárum.

Mirábiles elatiónes maris : * mirábilis in altis Dóminus.

Testimónia tua credibília facta sunt nimis :* domum tuam decet sanctitúdo, Domine, in longitúdinem diérum.

Glória Patri.

PSALMUS XCIX.

JUBILATE Deo, omnis terra;* servíte Dómino in lætítia.

Introíte in conspéctu ejus, * in exultatióne.

Scitóte quóniam Dóminus ipse est Deus :* ipse fecit nos, et non ipsi nos.

Pópulus ejus, et oves páscuæ ejus,* introíte portas ejus in confessióne, átria ejus in hymnis : confitémini illi.

Laudáte nomen ejus, quóniam suávis est Dóminus : in ætérnum misericórdia ejus,* et usque in generatiónem et generatiónem véritas ejus.

Glória Patri.

PSALMUS LXII.

DEUS, Deus meus,* ad te de luce vígilo.

Sítivit in te ánima mea,*

O Lord : the floods have lifted up their voice.

5 The floods have lifted up their waves : with the voices of many waters.

6 Wonderful are the surges of the sea : wonderful is the Lord on high.

7 Thy testimonies are made exceedingly credible : holiness becometh thy house, O Lord, unto length of days.

Glory, &c.

PSALM XCIX.

1 Sing joyfully unto God, all the earth : serve ye the Lord with gladness.

2 Come ye in before his presence : with exceeding joy.

3 Know ye that the Lord he is God : he hath made us, and not we ourselves.

4 We are his people, and the sheep of his pasture : go ye into his gates with thanksgiving, and into his courts with hymns ; give glory unto him.

5 Praise ye his name, for the Lord is gracious, his mercy is everlasting : and his truth endureth from generation to generation.

Glory, &c.

PSALM LXII.

1 O God, my God : to thee do I watch at break of day.

2 My soul hath thirsted for

quam multiplíciter tibi caro mea.

In terra desérta, et ínvia, et inaquósa;* sic in sancto appárui tibi, ut vidérem virtútem tuam, et glóriam tuam.

Quóniam mélior est misericórdia tua super vitas :* lábia mea laudábunt te.

Sic benedícam te in vita mea :* et in nómine tuo levábo manus meas.

Sicut ádipe et pinguédine repleátur ánima mea;* et lábiis exultatiónis laudábit os meum.

Si memor fui tui super stratum meum, in matutínis meditábor in te,* quia fuísti adjútor meus.

Et in velaménto alárum tuárum exultábo; adhǽsit ánima mea post te:* me suscépit déxtera tua.

Ipsi vero in vanum quæsiérunt ánimam meam ; introíbunt in inferióra terræ ;* tradéntur in manus gládii ; partes vúlpium erunt.

Rex vero lætábitur in Deo, laudabúntur omnes qui jurant in eo;* quia obstrúctum est os loquéntium iníqua.

Hic non dicitur Glória Patri.

thee : my flesh also, in ways how manifold.

3 In a desert and pathless land, where no water is : so have I appeared before thee in the sanctuary, that I might behold thy power and thy glory.

4 For thy mercy is better than many lives : my lips shall praise thee.

5 Thus will I bless thee all my life : and in thy name will I lift up my hands.

6 Let my soul be filled as with marrow and fatness : and my mouth shall praise thee with joyful lips.

7 If I have remembered thee upon my bed, in the morning will I meditate upon thee : for thou hast been my helper.

8 And under the cover of thy wings will I rejoice ; my soul hath cleaved unto thee : thy right hand hath upholden me.

9 But they have sought my soul in vain ; they shall go into the lower parts of the earth : they shall be delivered into the power of the sword, they shall be the portion of foxes.

10 But the king shall rejoice in God, all they shall be praised that swear by him : for the mouth of them that speak iniquity is stopped.

Gloria is not said here.

PSALMUS LXVI.

DEUS misereátur nostri, et benedícat nobis :* illúminet vultum suum super nos, et misereátur nostri.

Ut cognoscámus in terra viam tuam ;* in ómnibus géntibus salutáre tuum.

Confiteántur tibi pópuli, Deus ;* confiteántur tibi pópuli omnes.

Læténtur et exúltent gentes ;* quóniam júdicas pópulos in æquitáte, et gentes in terra dírigis.

Confiteántur tibi pópuli, Deus; confiteántur tibi pópuli omnes :* terra dedit fructum suum.

Benedícat nos Deus, Deus noster, benedícat nos Deus ;* et métuant eum omnes fines terræ.

Glória Patri.

CANTICUM TRIUM PUERORUM.

BENEDICITE, omnia ópera Dómini, Dómino ;* laudáte et superexaltáte eum in sæcula.

Benedícite, Angeli Dómini, Dómino :* benedícite, coeli, Dómino.

Benedícite, aquæ omnes quæ super coelos sunt, Dómino :* benedicite, omnes virtútes Dómini, Dómino.

Benedícite, sol et luna,

PSALM LXVI.

1 May God be merciful unto us, and bless us : may he cause the light of his countenance to shine upon us, and be merciful unto us.

2 That we may know thy way upon earth : thy salvation among all nations.

3 Let the people praise thee, O God : let all the people praise thee.

4 Let the nations rejoice and be glad : for thou judgest the people with equity, and rulest the nations upon earth.

5 Let the people praise thee, O God, let all the people praise thee : the earth hath given forth her fruit.

6 May God, even our God, bless us, may God bless us : and all the ends of the earth fear him.

Glory, &c.

THE BENEDICITE, OR SONG OF THE THREE CHILDREN.

1 O all ye works of the Lord, bless ye the Lord : praise and exalt him above all for ever.

2 O ye angels of the Lord, bless ye the Lord : bless the Lord, ye heavens.

3 O all ye waters that are above the heavens, bless ye the Lord : bless the Lord, all ye powers of the Lord.

4 O ye sun and moon, bless ye

Dómino:* benedícite, stellæ cœli, Dómino.

Benedícite, omnis imber et ros, Dómino:* benedícite, omnes spíritus Dei, Dómino.

Benedícite, ignis et æstus, Dómino:* benedícite, frigus et æstus, Dómino.

Benedícite, rores et pruína, Dómino:* benedícite, gelu et frigus, Dómino.

Benedícite, glacies et nives, Dómino: benedícite, noctes et dies, Dómino.

Benedícite, lux et ténebræ, Dómino:* benedícite, fúlgura et nubes, Dómino.

Benedícat terra Dóminum;* laudet et superexáltet eum in sæcula.

Benedícite, montes et colles, Dómino:* benedícite, univérsa germinántia in terra, Dómino.

Benedícite, fontes, Dómino:* benedícite, mária et flúmina, Dómino.

Benedícite, cete et ómnia quæ movéntur in aquis, Dómino:* benedícite, omnes vólucres cœli, Dómino.

Benedícite, omnes béstiæ et pécora, Dómino:* benedícite, fílii hóminum, Dómino.

Benedícat Israel Dóminum:* laudet et superexáltet eum in sæcula.

Benedícite, sacerdótes Dó-

the Lord : bless the Lord, ye stars of heaven.

5 O all ye showers and dew, bless ye the Lord: bless the Lord, all ye spirits of God.

6 O ye fire and heat, bless ye the Lord : bless the Lord, ye winter and summer.

7 O ye dews and hoar-frost, bless ye the Lord : bless the Lord, ye frost and cold.

8 O ye ice and snow, bless ye the Lord : bless the Lord, ye nights and days.

9 O ye light and darkness, bless ye the Lord : bless the Lord, ye lightnings and clouds.

10 O let the earth bless the Lord : let it praise and exalt him above all for ever.

11 O ye mountains and hills, bless ye the Lord : bless the Lord, all things that spring forth upon the earth.

12 O ye fountains, bless ye the Lord : bless the Lord, ye seas and floods.

13 O ye whales, and all that move in the waters, bless ye the Lord : bless the Lord, all ye fowls of the air.

14 O all ye beasts and cattle, bless ye the Lord : bless the Lord, ye sons of men.

15 Let Israel bless the Lord : let him praise and exalt him above all for ever.

16 O ye priests of the Lord,

mini, Dómino:* benedícite, servi Dómini, Dómino.

Benedícite, spíritus et ánimæ justórum, Dómino :* benedícite, sancti et húmiles corde, Domino.

Benedícite, Ananía, Azaría, Mísael, Domino:* laudáte et superexaltáte eum in sæcula.

Benedicámus Patrem, et Fílium, cum Sancto Spíritu;* laudémus et superexaltémus eum in sæcula.

Benedíctus es, Dómine, in firmaménto cœli;* et laudábilis, et gloriósus, et superexaltátus in sæcula.

Hic non dicitur Glória Patri.

L AUDATE Dóminum de cœlis,* laudáte eum in excélsis.

Laudáte eum, omnes Angeli ejus;* laudáte eum, omnes virtútes ejus.

Laudáte eum, sol et luna;* laudáte eum, omnes stellæ et lumen.

Laudáte eum, cœli cœlórum;* et aquæ omnes quæ super cœlos sunt, laudent nomen Domini.

Quia ipse dixit, et facta sunt;* ipse mandávit, et creáta sunt.

Státuit ea in ætérnum, et in sæculum sæculi:* præ-

bless ye the Lord: bless the Lord, ye servants of the Lord.

17 O ye spirits and souls of the just, bless ye the Lord : bless the Lord, all ye that are holy and humble of heart.

18 O Ananias, Azarias, Misael, bless ye the Lord: praise and exalt him above all for ever.

19 Let us bless the Father, and the Son, with the Holy Ghost: let us praise and exalt him above all for ever.

20 Blessed art thou, O Lord, in the firmament of heaven : worthy to be praised, and glorious, and exalted above all for ever.

Gloria *is not said here.*

1 Praise the Lord from the heavens: praise him in the heights.

2 Praise him, all his angels : praise him, all his hosts.

3 Praise him, sun and moon : praise him, all ye stars and light.

4 Praise him, O ye heaven of heavens: and let all the waters that are above the heavens praise the name of the Lord.

5 For he spake, and they were made: he commanded, and they were created.

6 He hath established them for ever, even for ever and ever :

céptum posuit, et non præteríbit.

Laudáte Dóminum de terra,* drácones, et omnes abyssi.

Ignis, grando, nix, glácies, spíritus procellárum;* quæ fáciunt verbum ejus.

Montes, et omnes colles;* ligna fructífera, et omnes cedri.

Béstiæ et univérsa pécora;* serpéntes, et vólucres pennátæ.

Reges terræ, et omnes pópuli;* príncipes, et omnes júdices terræ.

Júvenes et vírgines, senes cum junióribus, laudent nomen Dómini;* quia exaltátum est nomen ejus solíus.

Conféssio ejus super cœlum et terram;* et exaltávit cornu pópuli sui.

Hymnus ómnibus sanctis ejus;* fíliis Israel, pópulo appropinquánti sibi.

Hic non dicitur Glória Patri.

PSALMUS CXLIX.

CANTATE Dómino cánticum novum:* laus ejus in ecclésia Sanctórum.

Lætétur Israel in eo, qui fecit eum:* et fílii Sion exúltent in rege suo.

Laudent nomen ejus in

he hath made a decree, and it shall not pass away.

7 Praise the Lord from the earth: ye dragons and all deeps.

8 Fire and hail, snow and ice, and stormy winds: that fulfil his word.

9 Mountains and all hills: fruitful trees and all cedars.

10 Beasts and all cattle: creeping things and feathered fowls.

11 Kings of the earth and all people: princes and all judges of the earth.

12 Young men and maidens, old men and children, let them praise the name of the Lord: for his name alone is exalted.

13 His praise is above heaven and earth: and he hath exalted the horn of his people.

14 A song of praise to all his Saints: to the children of Israel, the people that draweth nigh unto him.

Gloria *is not said here.*

PSALM CXLIX.

1 Sing unto the Lord a new song: let his praise be in the church of the Saints.

2 Let Israel rejoice in him that made him: and the children of Sion be joyful in their king.

3 Let them praise his name in

choro;* in tympano et psal-
tério psallant ei.

Quia beneplácitum est Dó-
mino in pópulo suo:* et exaltábit mansuétos in salútem.

Exultábunt sancti in gló-
ria;* lætabúntur in cubíli-
bus suis.

Exaltatiónes Dei in gút-
ture eórum :* et gládii ancí-
pites in mánibus eórum.

Ad faciéndam vindíctam
in natiónibus :* increpatió-
nes in pópulis.

Ad alligándos reges eórum
in compédibus:* et nóbiles
eórum in mánicis férreis.

Ut fáciant in eis judícium
conscríptum:* glória hæc
est ómnibus sanctis ejus.

Hic non dicitur Glória
Patri.

the choir: let them sing unto
him with timbrel and psaltery.

4 For the Lord is well pleased
with his people: and will exalt
the meek unto salvation.

5 The Saints shall rejoice in
glory: they shall be joyful in
their beds.

6 The praises of God shall be
in their mouth: and two-edged
swords in their hands.

7 To execute vengeance upon
the nations: and chastisements
among the people.

8 To bind their kings with fetters: and their nobles with
chains of iron.

9 To execute upon them the
judgment that is written: this
glory have all his Saints.

Gloria *is not said here.*

PSALMUS CL.

LAUDATE Dóminum in
sanctis ejus:* laudáte
eum in firmaménto virtútis
ejus.

Laudáte eum in virtútibus
ejus:* laudáte eum secún-
dum multitúdinem magni-
túdinis ejus.

Laudáte eum in sono tu-
bæ:* laudáte eum in psal-
tério et cíthara.

Laudáte eum in tympano
et choro,* laudáte eum in
chordis et órgano.

Laudáte eum in cymbalis
bene sonántibus:laudáteeum

PSALM CL.

1 Praise the Lord in his holy
places: praise him in the firmament of his power.

2 Praise him in his mighty
acts: praise him according to
the multitude of his greatness.

3 Praise him with the sound
of the trumpet: praise him with
psaltery and harp.

4 Praise him with timbrel and
choir: praise him with strings
and organ.

5 Praise him upon the high-
sounding cymbals; praise him

In cymbalis jubilatiónis;*
omnis spíritus laudet Dóminum. Glória, &c.

Ant. Assúmpta est Ma-
ría in cœlum: gaudent An-
geli, laudántes benedícunt
Dóminum.

Capítulum. Cant. vi. —
Vidérunt eam fíliæ Sion,
et beatíssimam prædicavé-
runt, et regínæ laudavé-
runt eam.

R̲. Deo grátias.

HYMNUS.

O GLORIOSA Dómina,
　Excélsa super sídera,
Qui te creávit próvide,
Lactásti sacro úbere.

Quod Heva tristis ábstulit
Tu reddis almo gérmine:
Intrent ut astra flébiles,
Cœli fenéstra facta es.

Tu Regis alti jánua,
Et porta lucis fúlgida.
Vitam datam per Vírginem
Gentes redémptæ pláudite.

Glória tibi, Dómine,
Qui natus es de Vírgine,
Cum Patre, et Sancto Spí-
ritu,　　　[Amen.
In sempitérna sæcula.

V̲. Elégit eam Deus, et
præelégit eam.

R̲. Et habitáre eam facit
in tabernáculo suo.

Ant. O gloriósa.

upon cymbals of joy : let every
spirit praise the Lord.

Glory, &c.

Ant. Mary is taken up into
heaven : the angels rejoice and
praise the Lord.

Cant. vi. 8.

The daughters of Sion saw
her, and declared her most
blessed: and the queens praised
her.

R̲. Thanks be to God.

HYMN.

O Queen of all the virgin choir!
　Enthron'd above the starry
　sky!　　　[own breast
Who with pure milk from thy
Thy own Creator didst supply.

What man had lost in hapless
　Eve,　　　　　[stores;
Thy sacred womb to man re-
Thou to the wretched here be-
　neath　　　　　[doors.
Hast open'd Heaven's eternal

Hail, O refulgent Hall of light!
　Hail, Gate sublime of Heaven's
　high King!　　　[less life,
Through thee redeem'd to end-
Thy praise let all the nations
　sing.

O Jesu! born of Virgin bright,
　Immortal glory be to thee;
Praise to the Father infinite,
　And Holy Ghost eternally.
　　Amen.

V̲. God elected and pre-elected her.

R̲. And made her to dwell in
his tabernacle.

Ant. O glorious.

CANTICUM ZACHARIÆ.

BENEDICTUS Dóminus Deus Israel:* quia visitávit, et fecit redemptiónem plebis suæ.

Et eréxit cornu salútis nobis,* in domo David púeri sui.

Sicut locútus est per os sanctórum,* qui a sæculo sunt, Prophetárum ejus.

Salútem ex inimícis nostris,* et de manu ómnium qui odérunt nos.

Ad faciéndam misericórdiam cum pátribus nostris,* et memorári testaménti sui sancti.

Jusjurándum, quod jurávit ad Abraham patrem nostrum,* datúrum se nobis:

Ut sine timóre, de manu inimicórum nostrórum liberáti,* serviámus illi,

In sanctitáte et justítia coram ipso,* ómnibus diébus nostris.

Et tu, puer, Prophéta Altíssimi vocáberis;* præíbis enim ante fáciem Dómini, paráre vias ejus.

Ad dandam sciéntiam salútis plebi ejus;* in remissiónem peccatórum eórum.

Per víscera misericórdiæ Dei nostri;* in quibus visitávit nos óriens ex alto.

Illumináre his, qui in ténebris et in umbra mortis

CANTICLE OF ZACHARY.

1 Blessed be the Lord God of Israel : for he hath visited, and wrought the redemption of his people.

2 And hath raised up a horn of salvation to us : in the house of his servant David.

3 As he spake by the mouth of his holy prophets : who are from the beginning.

4 Salvation from our enemies : and from the hand of all that hate us.

5 To perform mercy to our fathers : and to remember his holy testament.

6 The oath that he sware to Abraham our father : that he would grant unto us :

7 That being delivered from the hands of our enemies : we may serve him without fear,

8 In holiness and justice before him : all the days of our life.

9 And thou, child, shalt be called the prophet of the Highest : for thou shalt go before the face of the Lord to prepare his ways.

10 To give knowledge of salvation unto his people : for the remission of their sins.

11 Through the bowels of the mercy of our God : whereby the orient from on high hath visited us.

12 To enlighten them that sit in darkness, and in the shadow

sedent;* ad dirigéndos pedes nostros in viam pacis.
Glória Patri.

Ad Benedictus. *Ant.*

O GLORIOSA Dei Geni-
trix virgo semper Maria,
quæ Dominum omnium me-
ruisti portare, et Regem An-
gelorum sola virgo lactare:
nostri, quæsumus, pia me-
morare, et pro nobis semper
Christum deprecare: ut tuis
fulti patrociniis, ad cœlestia
regna mereamur pervenire.

Oratio.

DEUS, qui de beatæ Ma-
riæ Virginis utero Ver-
bum tuum, Angelo nunti-
ante, carnem suscipere voluisti; præsta supplicibus
tuis, ut qui vere eam Genitricem Dei credimus, ejus
apud te intercessiónibus adjuvemur. Per eumdem
Dominum nostrum, Jesum
Christum.
R℣. Amen.
Ant. Virgo Maria, non est
tibi similis orta in mundo
inter mulieres: florens ut
rosa, fragrans sicut lilium:
ora pro nobis sancta Dei
Genitrix.
℣. Dignare me laudare te,
Virgo sacrata.
R℣. Da mihi virtutem con-
tra hostes tuos.

of death : to direct our feet into
the way of peace.
Glory, &c.

At Benedictus.

Ant. O glorious Mother of
God, Mary ever Virgin, who
alone hast merited to bear the
Lord of all things, and to nourish
from thy virginal breast the King
of Angels; remember us graciously, we beseech thee, and
ever intercede for us with Christ;
that, supported by thy patronage,
we may deserve to arrive at the
kingdom of heaven.

Prayer.

O God, who wast pleased that
thy Word, at the message of an
angel, should take flesh in the
womb of the blessed Virgin
Mary; grant to us, thy suppliants, that, as we believe her
to be truly the Mother of God,
so we may be assisted by her in-
tercessions with thee. Through
the same Christ our Lord.
R℣. Amen.
Ant. O Virgin Mary, there
hath not in the world, amongst
women, one arisen like unto
thee; blooming as the rose, fra-
grant as the lily : pray for us, O
holy Mother of God.
℣. Vouchsafe that I may
praise thee, O sacred Virgin.
R℣. Give me strength against
thy enemies.

Oratio.

BEATÆ et gloriosæ semperque virginis Mariæ, quæsumus Domine, intercessio gloriosa nos protegat, et ad vitam perducat æternam. Per Christum Dominum nostrum. R̂. Amen.

AD PRIMAM.
Ave Maria.

DEUS, in adjutórium meum inténde.

R̂. Dómine, ad adjuvándum me festína.

V̂. Glória Patri.

R̂. Sicut erat. Alleluia.

HYMNUS.

MEMENTO salútis Auctor, [poris,
Quod nostri quondam córEx illibáta Vírgine [seris.
Nascéndo, formam súmp-

Maria mater grátiæ,
Mater misericórdiæ,
Tu nos ab hoste prótege;
Et hora mortis súscipe.

Glória tibi, Dómine,
Qui natus es de Vírgine,
Cum Patre, et Sancto Spíritu, [Amen.
In sempitérna sæcula.

Ant. Assúmpta est.

PSALMUS LIIJ.

DEUS, in nómine tuo salvum me fac;* et in virtúte tua júdica me.

Prayer.

We beseech thee, O Lord, that the august intercession of the blessed and ever-glorious Virgin Mary may protect us, and conduct us to eternal life. Through Christ our Lord.

R̂. Amen.

PRIME.

Hail Mary.

V̂. O God, stretch forth unto mine aid.

R̂. O Lord, make haste to help me.

V̂. Glory, &c.

R̂. As it was, &c. Allel.

HYMN.

Remember, O thou Saviour Lord!
That in the Virgin's sacred womb [flesh
Thou wast conceiv'd, and of her
Didst our mortality assume.

Mother of grace, O Mary blest!
To thee, sweet fount of love, we fly: [us hence
Shield us through life, and take
To thy dear bosom when we die.

O Jesu! born of Virgin bright,
Immortal glory be to thee;
Praise to the Father infinite,
And Holy Ghost eternally.
Amen.

Ant. Mary was taken up.

PSALM LIII.

1 O God, save me in thy name : and judge me in thy strength.

Deus, exaúdi oratiónem meam ;* aúribus pércipe verba oris mei.

Quóniam alléni insurrexérunt advérsum me, et fortes quæsiérunt ánimam meam ;* et non proposuérunt Deum ante conspéctum suum.

Ecce enim Deus ádjuvat me ;* et Dóminus suscéptor est ánimæ meæ.

Avérte mala inimícis meis,* et in veritáte tua dispérde illos.

Voluntárie sacrificábo tibi,* et confitébor nómini tuo, Dómine; quóniam bonum est.

Quóniam ex omni tribulatióne eripuísti me ;* et super inimícos meos despéxit óculus meus.

Glória Patri.

2 O Lord, hear my prayer : and hearken to the words of my mouth.

3 For strangers have risen up against me, and the mighty have sought after my soul : and they have not set God before their eyes.

4 Behold, God is my helper : and the Lord upholdeth my soul.

5 Turn back the evil upon mine enemies : and destroy them in thy truth.

6 Freely will I sacrifice unto thee : and will praise thy name, O Lord, for it is good.

7 For thou hast delivered me out of all trouble : and mine eye hath looked down upon mine enemies.

Glory, &c.

PSALMUS CXVI.

LAUDATE Dóminum, omnes gentes ;* laudáte eum, omnes pópuli.

Quóniam confirmáta est super nos misericórdia ejus,* et véritas Dómini manet in ætérnum.

Glória Patri.

PSALM CXVI.

1 Praise the Lord, all ye gentiles : praise him, all ye people.

2 For his mercy is confirmed upon us : and the truth of the Lord endureth for ever.

Glory, &c.

PSALMUS CXVII.

CONFITEMINI Dómino quóniam bonus : * quóniam in sæculum misericórdia ejus.

Dicat nunc Israel, quó-

PSALM CXVII.

1 Give praise to the Lord, for he is good : for his mercy endureth for ever.

2 Let Israel now say, that he

niam bonus: * quóniam in sæculum misericórdia ejus.

Dicat nunc domus Aaron: * quóniam in sæculum misericórdia ejus.

Dicant nunc qui timent Dóminum: * quóniam in sæculum misericórdia ejus.

De tribulatióne invocávi Dóminum: * et exaudívit me in latitúdine Dóminus.

Dóminus mihi adjútor: * non timébo quid fáciat mihi homo.

Dóminus mihi adjútor: * et ego despíciam inimícos meos.

Bonum est confídere in Dómino,* quám confídere in hómine.

Bonum est speráre in Dómino, * quam speráre in princípibus.

Omnes gentes circuiérunt me: * et in nómine Dómini, quia ultus sum in eos.

Circumdántes circumdedérunt me: * et in nómine Dómini, quia ultus sum in eos.

Circumdedérunt me sicut apes, et exarsérunt sicut ignis in spinis: * et in nómine Dómini, quia ultus sum in eos.

Impúlsus evérsus sum ut cáderem: * et Dóminus suscépit me.

is good: that his mercy endureth for ever.

3 Let the house of Aaron now say: that his mercy endureth for ever.

4 Let them that fear the Lord now say: that his mercy endureth for ever.

5 In my trouble I called upon the Lord: and the Lord heard me, and enlarged me.

6 The Lord is my helper: I will not fear what man can do unto me.

7 The Lord is my helper: and I will look over my enemies.

8 It is good to trust in the Lord: rather than to have confidence in man.

9 It is good to trust in the Lord: rather than to have confidence in princes.

10 All nations compassed me about: and in the name of the Lord I have been revenged upon them.

11 Surrounding me they compassed me about: and in the name of the Lord I have been revenged upon them.

12 They surrounded me like bees, and they burned like fire among thorns: and in the name of the Lord I was revenged upon them.

13 Being pushed, I was overturned that I might fall: but the Lord upheld me.

Fortitúdo mea, et laus mea Dóminus:* et factus est mihi in salútem.

Vox exultaiónis, et salútis:* in tabernáculis justórum.

Déxtera Dómini fecit virtútem:* déxtera Dómini exaltávit me; déxtera Dómini fecit virtútem.

Non móriar, sed vivam:* et narrábo ópera Dómini.

Castigans castigávit me Dóminus: * et morti non trádidit me.

Aperíte mihi portas justítiæ, ingréssus in eas confitébor Dómino:* hæc porta Dómini, justi intrábunt in eam.

Confitébor tibi quóniam exaudísti me:* et factus es mihi in salútem.

Lápidem, quem reprobavérunt ædificántes: * hic factus est in caput ánguli.

A Dómino factum est istud:* et est mirábile in óculis nostris.

Hæc est dies, quam fecit Dóminus: * exultémus, et lætémur in ea.

O Dómine, salvum me fac: O Dómine, bene prosperáre: * benedíctus, qui venit in nómine Dómini.

14 The Lord is my strength and my praise : and he is become my salvation.

15 The voice of rejoicing and of salvation: is in the tabernacles of the just.

16 The right hand of the Lord hath wrought strength: the right hand of the Lord hath exalted me; the right hand of the Lord hath wrought strength.

17 I shall not die, but live : and shall declare the works of the Lord.

18 The Lord chastising hath chastised me: but he hath not delivered me over to death.

19 Open ye to me the gates of justice; I will go into them, and give praise to the Lord: this is the gate of the Lord, the just shall enter into it.

20 I will give glory to thee because thou hast heard me: and art become my salvation.

21 The stone which the builders rejected: the same is become the head of the corner.

22 This is the Lord's doing: and it is wonderful in our eyes.

23 This is the day which the Lord hath made: let us be glad and rejoice therein.

24 O Lord, save me: O Lord, give good success: blessed be he that cometh in the name of the Lord.

Benedíximus vobis de domo Dómini:* Deus Dóminus, et illúxit nobis.

Constitúite diem solémnem in condénsis, * usque ad cornu altáris.

Deus meus es tu, et confitébor tibi:* Deus meus es tu, et exaltábo te.

Confitébor tibi quóniam exaudísti me,* et factus es mihi in salútem.

Confitémini Dómino quóniam bonus:* quóniam in sæculum misericórdia ejus.

Glória Patri.

Ant. Assumpta est Maria in cœlum, gaudent Angeli, laudantes benedicunt Dominum.

Cap. Cant. vi.—Quæ est ista, quæ progréditur quasi auróra consúrgens, pulchra ut luna, elécta ut sol, terríbilis ut castrórum ácies ordináta?

℟. Sancta María Mater Christi,* audi rogántes sérvulos. Sancta.

℣. Et impetrátam nobis cœlítus tu defer indulgéntiam. Audi. Glória Patri. Sancta.

℣. Sancta Dei Génitrix,* Virgo semper María. Sancta.

℟. Intercéde pro nobis ad Dóminum Deum nostrum.

Oratio.

CONCEDE misericors Deus fragilitati nostræ præ-

. 25 We have blessed you out of the house of the Lord: the Lord is God, and he hath shone upon us.

26 Appoint a solemn day with shady boughs: even to the horn of the altar.

27 Thou art my God, and I will praise thee: thou art my God, and I will exalt thee.

28 I will praise thee because thou hast heard me: and art become my salvation.

29 O praise ye the Lord, for he is good: for his mercy endureth for ever.

Glory, &c.

Ant. Mary is taken up into heaven: the angels rejoice, and with praises bless the Lord.

Chap. Cant. vi.—Who is she that cometh forth as the morning rising, fair as the morn, bright as the sun,.terrible as an army set in array?

℟. Holy Mary, Mother of Christ,* give ear to thy suppliant servants.* Holy Mary, &c.

℣. And do thou vouchsafe to bring us the mercy we seek. Give ear, &c. Glory be, &c. Holy Mary, Mother of Christ.

℣. Holy Mother of God, Mary ever Virgin.

℟. Intercede for us with the Lord our God.

Prayer.

Vouchsafe to our weakness, O merciful God, the help of thy

sidium : ut qui sanctæ Dei
Genitricis memoriam agi-
mus; intercessionis ejus
auxílio, a nostris iniquitati-
bus resurgamus. Per eum-
dem Dominum, &c. &c.

Ant. Virgo Maria, &c. *ut
supra ad* Laudes, p. 35.

protection : that we who com-
memorate the holy Mother of
God, may, by the help of her
intercession, arise from our ini-
quities. Through the same
Christ our Lord. R̷. Amen.

Ant. O Virgin Mary, *as at*
Lauds, p. 35.

AD TERTIAM.

Ave Maria.

DEUS, in adjutórium
meum inténde.

R̷. Dómine, ad adjuván-
dum me festína.

℣. Glória Patri.

R̷. Sicut erat. Alleluia.

HYMNUS.

MEMENTO salútis Auc-
tor, &c., p. 36.

Ant. Maria Virgo.

PSALMUS CXIX.

AD Dóminum, cum tribu-
lárer, clamávi :* et ex-
audívit me.

Dómine, líbera ánimam
meam a lábiis iniquis,* et
a lingua dolósa.

Quid detur tibi, aut quid
apponátur tibi,* ad linguam
dolósam ?

Sagíttæ poténtis acútæ,*
cum carbónibus desolatóriis.

Heu mihi, quia incolátus
meus prolongátus est! Hab-
itávi cum habitántibus Ce-

TERCE.

Hail Mary.

℣. O God, stretch forth unto
mine aid.

R̷. O Lord, make haste to
help us.

℣. Glory, &c.

R̷. As it was, &c.   Alleluia.

HYMN.

Remember, O thou, p. 36.

Ant. The Virgin Mary.

PSALM CXIX.

1 When I was in trouble I
cried unto the Lord : and he
heard me.

2 O Lord, deliver my soul
from wicked lips : and from a
deceitful tongue.·

3 What can be given to thee,
or what can be superadded to
thee : unto a deceitful tongue?

4 Sharp arrows of the mighty
one : with desolating coals.

5 Wo is me, that my sojourn-
ing is prolonged ! I have dwelt
with the inhabitants of Cedar :

dar :* multum incola fuit ánima mea.

Cum his qui odérunt pacem, eram pacíficus :* cum loquébar illis, impugnábant me gratis.

Glória Patri.

PSALMUS CXX.

LEVAVI óculos meos in montes,* unde véniet auxílium mihi.

Auxílium meum a Dómino,* qui fecit cœlum et terram.

Non det in commotiónem pedem tuum ;* neque dormítet, qui custódit te.

Ecce non dormitábit, neque dórmiet,* qui custódit Israel.

Dóminus custódit te, Dóminus protéctio tua,* super manum déxteram tuam.

Per diem sol non uret te,* neque luna per noctem.

Dóminus custódit te ab omni malo :* custódiat ánimam tuam Dóminus.

Dóminus custódiat intróitum tuum et éxitum tuum,* ex hoc nunc, et usque in sæculum.

Glória Patri.

PSALMUS CXXI.

LÆTATUS sum in his quæ dicta sunt mihi :* in domum Dómini íbimus.

my soul hath been long a sojourner.

6 With them that hated peace, I was peaceable : when I spake unto them, they fought against me without a cause.

Glory, &c.

PSALM CXX.

1 I have lifted up mine eyes unto the hills : from whence shall come my help.

2 My help is from the Lord : who hath made heaven and earth.

3 Let him not suffer thy foot to be moved : neither let him sleep that keepeth thee.

4 Behold, he shall neither slumber nor sleep : that keepeth Israel.

5 The Lord is thy keeper, the Lord is thy defence : upon thy right hand.

6 The sun shall not burn thee by day : nor the moon by night.

7 The Lord preserveth thee from all evil : may the Lord preserve thy soul.

8 May the Lord preserve thy coming in and thy going out: from this time forth for evermore.

Glory, &c.

PSALM CXXI.

1 I was glad at the things that were said unto me : We will go into the house of the Lord.

Stantes erant pedes nostri,* in átriis tuis, Jerúsalem.

2 Our feet were wont to stand: in thy courts, O Jerusalem.

Jerúsalem, quæ ædificátur ut civitas,* cujus participátio ejus in idipsum.

3 Jerusalem, which is built as a city : that is at unity with itself.

Illuc enim ascendérunt tribus, tribus Dómini;* testimónium Israel ad confiténdum nómini Dómini.

4 For thither did the tribes go up, the tribes of the Lord : the testimony of Israel, to praise the name of the Lord.

Quia illic sedérunt sedes in judício,* sedes super domum David.

5 For there are set the seats of judgment : the seats over the house of David

Rogáte quæ ad pacem sunt, Jerúsalem,* et abundántia diligéntibus te.

6 Pray ye for the things that are for the peace of Jerusalem : and plenteousness be to them that love thee.

Fiat pax in virtúte tua,* et abundántia in túrribus tuis.

7 Let peace be in thy strength: and plenteousness in thy towers.

Propter fratres meos et próximos meos,* loquébar pacem de te.

8 For my brethren and companions' sake : I spake peace concerning thee.

Propter domum Dómini Dei nostri,* quæsivi bona tibi.

9 Because of the house of the Lord our God : I have sought good things for thee.

Glória Patri.

Glory, &c.

Ant. María Virgo assúmpta est ad æthéreum thálamum, in quo Rex regum stelláto sedet sólio.

Ant. Mary is taken up into the heavenly chamber, in which the King of kings sits upon his starry throne.

Cap. Eccli. xxiv.—Et sic in Sion firmáta sum, et in civitáte sanctificáta similiter requiévi, et in Jerúsalem potéstas mea.

Chap. Ecclus. xxiv.— And so was I established in Sion, and in the holy city likewise I rested, and my power was in Jerusalem.

℟. Deo grátias.

℟. Thanks be to God.

℟. Sancta Dei Génitrix,* Virgo semper, María Sancta.

℟. Holy Mother of God, Mary ever Virgin, Holy Mother of God.

℣. Intercéde pro nobis ad Dóminum Deum nostrum. Virgo. Glória Patri. Sancta.

℣. Post partum Virgo invioláta permansísti.

℞. Dei Génitrix, intercéde pro nobis.

Oratio.

DEUS, qui salutis æternæ, beatæ Mariæ virginitate fœcunda, humano generi præmia præstitisti; tribue, quæsumus, ut ipsam pro nobis intercedere sentiamus, per quam meruimus Auctorem vitæ suscipere, Dominum nostrum Jesum Christum Filium tuum, qui tecum vivit et regnat in unitate Spiritus Sancti Deus, per omnia sæcula sæculorum.

℞. Amen. Virgo Maria, &c., *ut supra ad* Laudes, p. 35.

AD SEXTAM.

Ave Maria.

DEUS, in adjutórium meum inténde.

℞. Dómine, ad adjuvándum me festína.

℣. Glória Patri.

℞. Sicut erat. Alleluia.

HYMNUS.

MEMENTO salútis Auctor. *Vide* p. 36.

Ant. In odórem.

℣. Intercede for us with the Lord our God. Mary ever Virgin, &c. Glory, &c. Holy Mother, &c.

℣. After childbirth thou remainest a pure Virgin.

℞. Mother of God, intercede for us.

Prayer.

O God, who, by the fruitful virginity of blessed Mary, hast bestowed upon mankind the rewards of eternal salvation; grant, we beseech thee, that we may feel her intercession for us, through whom we have been made worthy to receive the Author of life, our Lord Jesus Christ thy Son. Who livest and reignest, &c.

℞. Amen. O Virgin Mary, &c., *as at* Lauds, p. 35.

SEXT.

Hail Mary.

℣. O God, stretch forth unto mine aid.

℞. O Lord, make haste to help me.

℣. Glory, &c.

℞. As it was, &c. Alleluia.

HYMN.

Remember, &c. *as above*, p. 36.

Ant. We run.

PSALMUS CXXII.

A D te levávi óculos meos,*
qui hábitas in cœlis.

Ecce sicut óculi servó-
rum,* in mánibus dominó-
rum suórum.

Sicut óculi ancíllæ in mánibus dóminæ suæ,* ita
óculi nostri ad Dóminum
Deum nostrum, donec mise-
reátur nostri.

Miserére nostri, Dómine,
miserére nostri;* quia multum repléti sumus despec-
tióne.

Quia multum repléta est
ánima nostra :* oppróbrium
abundántibus, et despéctio
supérbis.   Glória Patri.

PSALMUS CXXIII.

N ISI quia Dóminus erat in
nobis, dicat nunc Israel:*
nisi quia Dóminus erat in
nobis.

Cum exúrgerent hómines
in nos,* forte vivos deglu-
tíssent nos.

Cum irascerétur furor
eórum in nos,* fórsitan
aqua absorbuísset nos.

Torréntem   pertransívit
ánima   nostra :*   fórsitan
pertransísset ánima nostra
aquam intolerábilem.

Benedíctus   Dóminus,*
qui non dedit nos in cap-
tiónem déntibus eórum.

PSALM CXXII.

1 Unto thee have I lifted up
mine eyes : who dwellest in the
heavens.

2 Behold as the eyes of servants : are on the hands of their
masters ;

3 As the eyes of the maiden
are on the hands of her mis-
tress : even so are our eyes unto
the Lord our God, until he have
mercy upon us.

4 Have mercy upon us, O
Lord, have mercy upon us: for
we are greatly filled with contempt.

5 Yea, our soul is greatly
filled : we are an offence unto
the wealthy, and a contempt unto
the proud.   Glory, &c.

PSALM CXXIII.

1 Unless the Lord had been
with us, now may Israel say:
unless the Lord had been with
us.

2 When men rose up against
us : peradventure they had swallowed us up alive.

3 When their fury was en-
kindled against us : peradventure the waters had swallowed
us up.

4 Our soul passed through a
torrent : peradventure our soul
would have passed through waters insupportable.

5 Blessed be the Lord : who
hath not given us over for a prey
unto their teeth.

Anima nostra sicut passer erépta est* de láqueo venántium.

Láqueus contrítus est,* et nos liberáti sumus.

Adjutórium nostrum in nómine Dómini,* qui fecit cœlum et terram. Glória.

PSALMUS CXXIV.

QUI confídunt in Dómino, sicut mons Sion :* non commovébitur in ætérnum, qui hábitat in Jerúsalem.

Montes in circúitu ejus ;* et Dóminus in circúitu pópuli sui, ex hoc nunc, et usque in sæculum.

Quia non relínquet Dóminus virgam peccatórum super sortem justórum ;* ut non exténdant justi ad iniquitátem manus suas.

Bénefac, Dómine, bonis,* et rectis corde.

Declinántes autem in obligatiónes, addúcet Dóminus cum operántibus iniquitátem :* pax super Israel. Glória Patri.

Ant. In odórem unguentórum tuórum cúrrimus; adolescéntulæ dilexérunt te nimis.

Cap. Eccli. xxiv.

ET radicávi in pópulo honorificáto, et in parte Dei mei hæréditas illíus,

6 Our soul hath been snatched as a sparrow : out of the snare of the fowlers.

7 The snare is broken : and we are delivered.

8 Our help is in the name of the Lord : who hath made heaven and earth. Glory, &c.

PSALM CXXIV.

1 They who trust in the Lord shall be as Mount Sion : he shall not be moved for ever that dwelleth in Jerusalem.

2 The hills are round about her : even so is the Lord round about his people, from this time forth for evermore.

3 For the Lord will not leave the rod of sinners upon the lot of the just : that the just stretch not forth their hands to iniquity.

4 Do well, O Lord, to those that are good : and to the right of heart.

5 But such as turn aside unto deceits, the Lord shall number with the workers of iniquity : peace upon Israel.

Glory, &c.

Ant. We run to the odour of thy ointments : the young maidens have loved thee exceedingly.

Chap. Ecclus. xxiv.—And I took root in an honourable people, and in the portion of my God his inheritance : and my

et in plenitúdine sanctó-
rum deténtio mea.

℟. Deo grátias.

℟. Post partum Virgo*
invioláta permansísti. Post
partum.

℣. Dei Génitrix, intercéde
pro nobis. Inviolata. Glória.
Post partum.

℣. Speciósa facta es, et
suavis.

℟. In delíciis tuis, sancta
Dei Génitrix.

Oratio.

DEUS, qui virginalem au-
lam beátæ Mariæ vir-
ginis, in qua habitares, eligere dignatus es; da quæ-
sumus, ut sua nos defen-
sione munitos, jucundos
suæ facias interesse com-
memorationi. Qui vivis et
regnas, &c.

Et cetera, ut supra ad
Laudes, p. 35.

AD NONAM.
Ave Maria.

DEUS, in adjutórium me-
um inténde.

℟. Dómine, ad adjuván-
dum me festína.

℣. Glória Patri.

℟. Sicut erat. Alleluia.

HYMNUS.

MEMENTO salútis Auc-
tor. *Vide* p. 36.

Ant. Pulchra es.

abode is in the full assembly of
Saints.

℟. Thanks be to God.

℟. After childbirth thou remainest a pure Virgin. After,
&c.

℣. Mother of God, intercede
for us. Thou remainest. Glory.
After childbirth.

℣. Thou art become beautiful
and sweet.

℟. In thy delights, O holy
Mother of God.

Prayer.

O God, who didst vouchsafe
to choose the virginal womb of
the blessed Virgin Mary as thy
habitation; grant us, we beseech
thee, that, fortified by her protection, we may joyfully assist
at her commemoration. Who
livest and reignest world without end. Amen.

O Virgin Mary, &c., *as at*
Lauds, p. 35.

NONE.
Hail Mary.

℣. O God, stretch forth unto
mine aid.

℟. O Lord, make haste to help
me.

℣. Glory, &c.

℟. As it was, &c.   Alleluia.

HYMN.

Remember, &c., *as above,*
p. 36.

Ant. Thou art fair.

IN converténdo Dóminus captivitátem Sion,* facti sumus sicut consoláti.

Tunc replétum est gáudio os nostrum,* et lingua nostra exultatióne.

Tunc dicent inter gentes:* Magnificávit Dóminus fácere cum eis.

Magnificávit Dóminus fácere nobiscum:* facti sumus lætántes.

Convérte, Dómine, captivitátem nostram,* sicut torrens in Austro.

Qui séminant in lácrymis,* in exultatióne metent.

Eúntes ibant et flebant,* mitténtes sémina sua.

Veniéntes autem vénient cum exultatióne,* portántes manípulos suos.

Glória Patri.

NISI Dóminus ædificáverit domum,* in vanum laboravérunt qui ædificant eam.

Nisi Dóminus custodierit civitátem,* frustra vígilat qui custódit eam.

Vanum est vobis ante lucem súrgere :* súrgite postquam sedéritis, qui manducátis panem dolóris.

Cum déderit diléctis suis

1 When the Lord turned again the captivity of Sion : we became like men that are comforted.

2 Then was our mouth filled with gladness : and our tongue with joy.

3 Then shall they say among the gentiles : The Lord hath done great things for them.

4 The Lord hath done great things for us : we are become very joyful.

5 Turn again our captivity, O Lord : as a river in the south.

6 They that sow in tears : shall reap in joy.

7 Going on their way they went and wept : scattering their seed.

8 But returning they shall come with joyfulness : bringing their sheaves with them.

Glory, &c.

1 Unless the Lord build the house : they labour in vain that build it.

2 Unless the Lord keep the city : he watcheth in vain that keepeth it.

3 In vain ye rise before the light : rise not till ye have rested, O ye that eat the bread of sorrow.

4 When he hath given sleep

somnum :* ecce hæréditas Dómini, fílii; merces, fructus ventris.

Sicut sagíttæ in manu poténtis,* ita fílii excussórum.

Beátus vir, qui implévit desidérium suum ex ipsis :* non confundétur, cum loquétur inimícis suis in porta. Glória Patri.

PSALMUS CXXVII.

BEATI omnes, qui timent Dóminum ;* qui ámbulant in viis ejus.

Labóres mánuum tuárum quia manducábis,* beátus es, et bene tibi erit.

Uxor tua sicut vitis abúndans,* in latéribus domus tuæ.

Fílii tui sicut novéllæ olivárum,* in circúitu mensæ tuæ.

Ecce sic benedicétur homo,* qui timet Dóminum.

Benedícat tibi Dóminus ex Sion ;* et vídeas bona Jerúsalem, ómnibus diébus vitæ tuæ.

Et vídeas fílios filiórum tuórum,* pacem super Israel. Glória Patri.

Ant. Pulchra es et decóra, fília Jerúsalem ; terríbilis ut castrórum ácies ordináta.

to his beloved : lo, children are an heritage from the Lord, and the fruit of the womb a reward.

5 Like as arrows in the hand of the mighty one : so are the children of those who have been cast out.

6 Blessed is the man whose desire is satisfied with them : he shall not be confounded, when he speaketh with his enemies in the gate. Glory, &c.

PSALM CXXVII.

1 Blessed are all they that fear the Lord : that walk in his ways.

2 For thou shalt eat the labours of thy hands : blessed art thou, and it shall be well with thee.

3 Thy wife shall be as a fruitful vine : on the walls of thy house.

4 Thy children as olive-plants : round about thy table.

5 Behold, thus shall the man be blessed : that feareth the Lord.

6 May the Lord bless thee out of Sion : and mayest thou see the good things of Jerusalem all the days of thy life.

7 And mayest thou see thy children's children : peace upon Israel. Glory, &c.

Ant. Thou art fair and comely, O daughter of Jerusalem : terrible as an army set in array.

Cap. *Eccll.* xxiv.—In platéis sicut cinnamómum et bálsamum aromátizans, odórem dedi ; quasi myrrha elécta, dedi suavitátem odóris.

℞. Deo grátias.

℞. Speciósa facta es,* et suavis. Speciosa.

℣. In delíciis tuis sancta Dei Génitrix. Et suavis. Glória Patri. Speciósa, &c.

℣. Elégit eam Deus, et præelégit eam.

℞. Et habitáre eam facit in tabernáculo suo.

Oratio.

FAMULORUM tuorum, quæsumus, Domine, delictis ignosce ; ut qui tibi placere de actibus nostris non valemus, Genitricis Filii tui Domini nostri intercessione salvemur. Qui tecum vivit et regnat in unitate Spiritus Sancti Deus, per omnia sæcula sæculorum.

℞. Amen. *Et cetera ut supra ad* Laudes.

AD VESPERAS.

Ave Maria.

DEUS, in adjutórium meum inténde.

℞. Dómine, ad adjuvándum me festína.

℣. Glória Patri.

℞. Sicut erat. Alleluía.

Chap. *Ecclus.* xxiv.—In the streets, like cinnamon and aromatic balm, I gave forth a sweet fragrance : like the choicest myrrh, I yielded a sweetness of odour.

℞. Thanks be to God.

℞. Thou art become beautiful and sweet. Thou art become, &c.

℣. In thy delights, O holy Mother of God. And sweet. Glory. Thou art become, &c.

℣. God hath elected and pre-elected her.

℞. And made her to dwell in his tabernacle.

Prayer.

Forgive, O Lord, we beseech thee, the offences of thy servants ; that we, who are unable to please thee by our own acts, may be saved by the intercession of the Mother of thy Son Jesus Christ our Lord, who liveth and reigneth, &c.

℞. Amen, &c., *as at* Lauds.

AT VESPERS.

Hail Mary.

℣. O God, stretch forth unto mine aid.

℞. O Lord, make haste to help me.

℣. Glory, &c.

℞. As it was, &c. Alleluia.

A Septuag. usque ad Feriam v. in cœna Domini, loco Alleluia dicitur :

Laus tibi, Domine, Rex æternæ gloriæ.

Ant. Beata mater.

From Vespers on Saturday before Septuag· sima Sunday till None on Easter Saturday, instead of Alleluia is said :

Praise be to thee, O Lord, King of eternal glory.

Ant. Blessed Mother.

PSALMUS CIX.

DIXIT Dóminus Dómino meo :* Sede a dextris meis.

Donec ponam inimícos tuos,* scabéllum pedum tuórum.

Virgam virtútis tuæ emíttet Dóminus ex Sion ;* domináre in médio inimicórum tuórum.

Tecum princípium in die virtútis tuæ, in splendóribus Sanctórum :* ex útero ante lucíferum génui te.

Jurávit Dóminus, et non pœnitébit eum :* Tu es sacérdos in ætérnum, secúndum órdinem Melchísedech.

Dóminus a dextris tuis,* confrégit in die iræ suæ reges.

Judicábit in natiónibus, implébit ruínas :* conquassábit cápita in terra multórum.

De torrénte in via bibet :* proptérea exaltábit caput.

Glória Patri.

PSALM CIX.

1 The Lord said to my Lord : Sit thou at my right hand :

2 Until I make thine enemies : thy footstool.

3 The Lord shall send forth the rod of thy power from out of Sion : rule thou in the midst of thine enemies.

4 Thine shall be the dominion in the day of thy power, amid the brightness of the Saints : from the womb, before the day-star, have I begotten thee.

5 The Lord hath sworn, and will not repent : Thou art a priest for ever according to the order of Melchisedec.

6 The Lord upon thy right hand : hath overthrown kings in the day of his wrath.

7 He shall judge among the nations, he shall fulfil destructions : he shall smite in sunder the heads in the land of many.

8 He shall drink of the brook in the way : therefore shall he lift up his head.   Glory, &c.

PSALMUS CXII.

LAUDATE, púeri, Dómi-
num;* laudáte nomen
Dómini.

Sit nomen Dómini bene-
díctum,* ex hoc nunc, et
usque in sæculum.

A solis ortu usque ad oc-
cásum,* laudábile nomen
Dómini.

Excélsus super omnes
gentes Dóminus,* et super
cœlos glória ejus.

Quis sicut Dóminus Deus
noster, qui in altis hábitat,*
et humília réspicit in cœlo
et in terra?

Súscitans a terra íno-
pem,* et de stércore érigens
paúperem.

Ut cóllocet eum cum
princípibus,* cum princípibus pópuli sui.

Qui habitáre facit stéri-
lem in domo,* matrem filiórum lætántem.

Glória Patri.

PSALMUS CXXI.

LÆTATUS sum in his
quæ dicta sunt mihi :*
in domum Dómini íbimus.

Stantes erant pedes nos-
tri * in átriis tuis, Jerúsalem.

Jerúsalem, quæ ædificá-
tur ut cívitas,* cujus participátio ejus in idípsum.

Illuc enim ascendérunt

PSALM CXII.

1 Praise the Lord, ye children :
praise ye the name of the Lord.

2 Blessed be the name of the
Lord : from this time forth for
evermore.

3 From the rising up of the
sun unto the going down of the
same : the name of the Lord is
worthy to be praised.

4 The Lord is high above all
nations : and his glory above
the heavens.

5 Who is like unto the Lord
our God, who dwelleth on high :
and regardeth the things that
are lowly in heaven and in
earth?

6 Who raiseth up the needy
from the earth : and lifteth the.
poor from off the dunghill :

7 That he may set him with
the princes : even with the
princes of his people.

8 Who maketh the barren
woman to dwell in her house :
the joyful mother of children.

Glory, &c.

PSALM CXXI.

1 I was glad at the things that
were said unto me : We will go
into the house of the Lord.

2 Our feet were wont to stand :
in thy courts, O Jerusalem.

3 Jerusalem, which is built
as a city : that is at unity with
itself.

4 For thither did the tribes go

tribus, tribus Dómini;* testimónium Israel, ad confiténdum nómini Dómini.

Quia illic sedérunt sedes in judício,* sedes super domum David.

Rogáte quæ ad pacem sunt, Jerúsalem ;* et abundántia diligéntibus te.

Fiat pax in virtúte tua,* et abundántia in túrribus tuis.

Propter fratres meos et próximos meos,* loquébar pacem de te.

Propter domum Dómini Dei nostri,* quæsívi bona tibi.

Glória Patri.

PSALMUS CXXVI.

NISI Dóminus ædificáverit domum, * in vanum laboravérunt qui ædíficant eam.

Nisi Dóminus custodíerit civitátem, * frustra vígilat qui custódit eam.

Vanum est vobis ante lucem súrgere : * súrgite postquam sedéritis, qui manducátis panem dolóris.

Cum déderit diléctis suis somnum: * ecce hæréditas Dómini, fílii; merces, fructus ventris.

Sicut sagíttæ in manu poténtis, * ita fílii excussórum.

up, the tribes of the Lord : the testimony of Israel, to praise the name of the Lord.

5 For there are set the seats of judgment : the seats over the house of David.

6 Pray ye for the things that are for the peace of Jerusalem : and plenteousness be to them that love thee.

7 Let peace be in thy strength : and plenteousness in thy towers.

8 For my brethren and companions' sake : I spake peace concerning thee.

9 Because of the house of the Lord our God : I have sought good things for thee.

Glory, &c.

PSALM CXXVI.

1 Unless the Lord build the house : they labour in vain that build it.

2 Unless the Lord keep the city : he watcheth in vain that keepeth it.

3 In vain ye rise before the light : rise not till ye have rested, O ye that eat the bread of sorrow.

4 When he hath given sleep to his beloved : lo, children are an heritage from the Lord, and the fruit of the womb a reward.

5 Like as arrows in the hand of the mighty one : so are the children of those who have been cast out.

Beátus vir, qui implévit desidérium suum ex ipsis :* non confundétur, cum loquétur inimícis suis in porta.

Glória Patri.

PSALMUS CXLVII.

LAUDA, Jerúsalem, Dóminum;* lauda Deum tuum, Sion.

Quóniam confortávit seras portárum tuárum :* benedíxit fíliis tuis iu te.

Qui pósuit fines tuos pacem ;* et ádipe fruménti sátiat te.

Qui emíttit elóquium suum terræ :* velóciter currit sermo ejus.

Qui dat nivem sicut lanam :* nébulam sicut cínerem spargit.

Mittit crystállum suum sicut buccéllas :* ante fáciem frigoris ejus quis sustinébit ?

Emittet verbum suum, et liquefáciet ea :* flabit spíritus ejus, et fluent aquæ.

Qui annúntiat verbum suum Jacob,* justitias et judícia sua Israel.

Non fecit táliter omni natióni ;* et judícia sua non manifestávit eis.

Glória Patri.

Ant. Beáta Mater, et intácta virgo, glorióso regína

6 Blessed is the man whose desire is satisfied with them : he shall not be confounded, when he speaketh with his enemies in the gate.

Glory, &c.

PSALM CXLVII.

1 Praise the Lord, O Jerusalem: praise thy God, O Sion.

2 For he hath strengthened the bars of thy gates : he hath blessed thy children within thee.

3 He hath made peace within thy borders : and filleth thee with the fatness of corn.

4 He sendeth forth his commandment on the earth : his word runneth very swiftly.

5 He giveth snow like wool : he scattereth the hoar-frost like ashes.

6 He sendeth his ice like morsels : who is able to abide his frost ?

7 He shall send forth his word, and melt them : he shall blow with his wind, and the waters shall flow.

8 He maketh known his word unto Jacob: his statutes and ordinances unto Israel.

9 He hath not dealt so with any nation: neither hath he shewed them his judgments.

Glory, &c.

Ant. Blessed Mother, and Virgin inviolate, glorious Queen of

mundi, intercéde pro nobis ad Dóminum.

Cap. Eccli. xxiv.—Ab initio et ante sæcula creata sum, et usque ad futurum sæculum non desinam ; et in habitatione sancta coram ipso ministravi.

℟. Deo grátias.

HYMNUS.

AVE, maris stella,
   Dei Mater alma,
Atque semper Virgo,
Felix cœli porta.

Sumens illud Ave
Gabriélis ore,
Funda nos in pace,
Mutans Hevæ nomen.

Solve vincla reis,
Profer lumen cæcis
Mala nostra pelle,
Bona cuncta posce.

Monstra te esse matrem,
Sumat per te preces,
Qui pro nobis natus,
Tulit esse tuus.

Virgo singuláris,
Inter omnes mitis,
Nos culpis solútos,
Mites fac et castos.

Vitam præsta puram,
Iter para tutum,
Ut vidéntes Jesum,
Semper collætémur.

Sit laus Deo Patri,
Summo Christo decus,

the world, intercede for us with the Lord.

Chap. Ecclus. xxiv. — From the beginning, and before the world, was I created, and unto the world to come I shall not cease to be, and in the holy dwelling-place I have ministered before him.

℟. Thanks be to God.

HYMN.

Hail, thou Star of ocean !
   Portal of the sky !
Ever Virgin Mother
   Of the Lord most high !

Oh ! by Gabriel's Ave,
   Utter'd long ago,
Eva's name reversing,
   Stablish peace below.

Break the captive's fetters ;
   Light on blindness pour ;
All our ills expelling,
   Every bliss implore.

Shew thyself a Mother ;
   Offer him our sighs,
Who for us incarnate
   Did not thee despise.

Virgin of all virgins !
   To thy shelter take us :
Gentlest of the gentle !
   Chaste and gentle make us.

Still, as on we journey,
   Help our weak endeavour,
Till with thee and Jesus
   We rejoice for ever.

Through the highest heaven,
   To the Almighty Three,

Siprítui Sancto,
Tribus honor unus.

℣. Ora pro nobis, sancta
Dei Génitrix.

℟. Ut digni efficiamur
promissiónibus Christi.

Ant. Sancta Maria.

CANTICUM B. MARIÆ
VIRGINIS.
Lucæ i.

MAGNIFICAT * ánima
mea Dóminum.

Et exultávit spíritus me-
us* in Deo salutári meo.

Quia respéxit humilitátem
ancíllæ suæ :* ecce enim ex
hoc beátam me dicent om-
nes generatiónes.

Quia fecit mihi magna,
qui potens est ;* et sanctum nomen ejus.

Et misericórdia ejus a
progénie in progénies,* ti-
méntibus eum.

Fecit poténtiam in bráchio
suo ;* dispérsit supérbos
mente cordis sui.

Depósuit poténtes de
sede,* et exaltávit húmiles.

Esuriéntes implévit bo-
nis,* et dívites dimísit iná-
nes.

Suscépit Israel púerum
suum,* recordátus miseri-
córdiæ suæ.

Father, Son, and Spirit,
One same glory be. Amen.

℣ Pray for us, O holy Mother
of God.

℟. That we may be made
worthy of the promises of Christ.

Ant. Holy Mary.

THE MAGNIFICAT, OR SONG OF
THE B.V.M.
Luke i.

1 My soul doth magnify : the
Lord.

2 And my spirit hath rejoiced :
in God my Saviour.

3 For he hath regarded the
lowliness of his handmaid : for
behold from henceforth all generations shall call me blessed.

4 For he that is mighty hath
done great things unto me : and
holy is his name.

5 And his mercy is from generation to generation : unto
them that fear him.

6 He hath shewed strength
with his arm : he hath scattered
the proud in the imagination of
their heart.

7 He hath put down the
mighty from their seat : and
hath exalted the humble.

8 He hath filled the hungry
with good things : and the rich
he hath sent empty away.

9 He hath upholden his servant Israel : being mindful of
his mercy.

Sicut locútus est ad pa-
tres nostros;* Abraham, et
sémini ejus in sæcula.

Glória Patri.

Ad Magnificat.

Ant. Sancta Maria, suc-
curre miseris; juva pusil-
lanimes: refove flebiles:
ora pro populo: intervent
pro clero: intercede pro
devoto femineo sexu.

Oratio.

CONCEDE nos famulos
tuos quæsumus, Do-
mine Deus, perpetua mentis
et corporis sanitate gaudere;
et gloriosa beatæ Mariæ
semper Virginis interces-
sione a præsenti liberari tris-
titia, et æterna perfrui læ-
titia. Per Dominum nos-
trum Jesum, &c.

R̃. Amen. *Et cetera ut
supra ad* Laudes.

*Quando Offic. B. V. dicitur
cum Officio diei, Comple-
torium B. V. incipiatur
post benedictionem de Completorio diei.*

AD COMPLETORIUM.

Ave Maria, &c.

CONVERTE nos, Deus
salutáris noster,

R̃. Et avérte iram tuam
a nobis.

10 As he spake unto our fathers : to Abraham and his seed
for ever.

Glory, &c.

At the Magnificat.

Ant. Holy Mary, succour the
afflicted, help the fainthearted,
comfort the sorrowing, pray for
the people, intercede for the
clergy, and for the devout female sex.

Prayer.

Vouchsafe, O Lord God, we
beseech thee, to us, thy servants,
that we may enjoy perpetual
health of mind and body ; and
by the glorious intercession of
blessed Mary ever Virgin, may
be delivered from present sad-
ness, and come to the fruition of
eternal joys. Through our Lord
Jesus Christ.

R̃. Amen, &c., *as at* Lauds.

*When the Offic. B. V. is said with
the Office of the day, the Compline of B. V. begins after the
blessing of the Compline of the
day.*

COMPLINE.

Hail Mary.

V̄. Convert thou us, O God
our Saviour.

R̃. And turn away thine anger
from us.

℣. Deus, in adjutórium meum inténde.

℟. Dómine, ad adjuvándum me festína.

℣. Glória Patri.

℟. Sicut erat. Allelúia.

Ant. Cum jucunditáte.

PSALMUS XII.

USQUEQUO, Dómine, obliviscéris me in finem?* Usquequo avértis fáciem tuam a me?

Quámdiu ponam consília in ánima mea, * dolórem in corde meo per diem?

Usquequo exaltábitur inimícus meus super me? * réspice, et exáudi me, Dómine Deus meus.

Illúmina oculos meos, ne umquam obdórmiam in morte:* nequándo dicat inimícus meus: Præválui advérsus eum.

Qui tríbulant me, exaltábunt, si motus fúero:* ego autem in misericórdia tua sperávi.

Exultábit cor meum in salutári tuo : cantábo Dómino,qui bona tríbuit mihi :* et psallam nómini Dómini altíssimi.

Glória Patri.

PSALMUS XLII.

JUDICA me, Deus, et discérne causam meam de gente non sancta :* ab hómine iníquo, et dolóso érue me.

℣. O God, stretch forth unto mine aid.

℟. O Lord, make haste to help me.

℣. Glory, &c.

℟. As it was, &c. Allelúia.

Ant. With joyfulness.

PSALM XII.

1 How long, O Lord, wilt thou forget me unto the end : how long dost thou turn away thy face from me?

2 How long shall I take counsels in my soul: and sorrow in my heart all the day?

3 How long shall my enemy be exalted over me: consider and hear me, O Lord my God.

4 Enlighten my eyes, that I may never sleep in death: lest at any time my enemy say, I have prevailed against him.

5 They that troubled me will rejoice when I am moved: but I have trusted in thy mercy.

6 My heart shall rejoice in thy salvation; I will sing to the Lord, who giveth me good things : yea, I will sing to the name of the Lord the Most High.

Glory, &c.

PSALM XLII.

1 Judge me, O God, and distinguish my cause from the nation that is not holy: deliver me from the unjust and deceitful man.

Quia tu es Deus fortitúdo mea : * quare me repulísti, et quare tristis incédo, dum afflígit me inimícus?

Emítte lucem tuam, et veritátem tuam : * ipsa me deduxérunt, et adduxérunt in montem sanctum tuum, et in tabernácula tua.

Et introíbo ad altáre Dei : * ad Deum, qui lætíficat juventútem meam.

Confitébor tibi in cíthara, Deus, Deus meus : * quare tristis es ánima mea, et quare contúrbas me?

Spera in Deo, quóniam adhuc confitébor illi,* salutáre vultus mei, et Deus meus.

Glória Patri.

PSALMUS CXXVIII.

S ÆPE expugnavérunt me a juventúte mea ; * dicat nunc Israel.

Sæpe expugnavérunt me a juventúte mea ; * étenim non potuérunt mihi.

Supra dorsum meum fabricavérunt peccatóres : * prolongavérunt iniquitátem suam.

Dóminus justus concídit cervíces peccatórum :* confundántur, et convertántur retrórsum omnes, qui odérunt Sion.

Fiant sicut fœnum tectó-

2 For thou, O God, art my strength : why hast thou cast me off? and why do I go sorrowful whilst the enemy afflicteth me?

3 Send forth thy light and thy truth : they have conducted me and brought me unto thy holy mount, and into thy tabernacles.

4 And I will go unto the altar of God : to God, who giveth joy to my youth.

5 I will praise thee on the harp, O God, my God : why art thou sorrowful, O my soul? and why dost thou disquiet me?

6 Hope in God, for I will still give praise to him : who is the salvation of my countenance, and my God.

Glory, &c.

PSALM CXXVIII.

1 Many a time have they fought against me from my youth : let Israel now say.

2 Many a time have they fought against me from my youth up : but they could not prevail against me.

3 The wicked have wrought upon my back : and prolonged their iniquity.

4 The just Lord hath hewn asunder the necks of sinners : let all them be confounded and turned back, that have hated Sion.

5 Let them be as grass upon

rum : * quod priúsquam e-
vellátur, exáruit:

De quo non implévit ma-
num suam, qui metit,* et
sinum suum, qui manípu-
los cólligit.

Et non dixérunt, qui præ-
teríbant : Benedíctio Dó-
mini super vos :* benedíximus vobis in nómine Dó-
mini.

Glória Patri.

DOMINE non est exaltá-
tum cor meum :* neque
eláti sunt óculi mei.

Neque ambulávi in mag-
nis, * neque in mirabílibus
super me.

Si non humíliter sentié-
bam :* sed exaltávi ánimam
meam.

Sicut ablactátus est super
matre sua, * ita retribútio
in ánima mea.

Speret Israel in Dómino,*
ex hoc nunc, et usque in
sæculum.

Glória Patri.

Ant. Cum jucunditáte me-
móriam beátæ Maríæ cele-
brémus : ut ipsa pro nobis
intercédat ad Dóminum Je-
sum Christum.

Cap. Ecclus. xxiv. — Ego
Mater pulchræ dilectionis,
et timoris, et agnitionis, et
sanctæ spei.

℟. Deo grátias.

the tops of houses : that wither-
eth before it be plucked up.

6 Wherewith the mower filleth not his hand: nor he that
gathereth the sheaves his bosom.

7 And they who pass by say
not, The blessing of the Lord be
upon you: we have blessed you
in the name of the Lord.

Glory, &c.

1 Lord, my heart is not lifted
up : nor are mine eyes lofty.

2 Neither have I walked in
great matters : nor in things too
wonderful for me.

3 If I have not been humbly
minded : but have lifted up my
soul ;

4 As a child that is weaned
upon his mother's breast: so let
my reward be in my soul.

5 Let Israel hope in the Lord :
from this time forth for evermore.

Glory, &c.

Ant. With joyfulness we celebrate the memory of blessed
Mary ; that she may intercede
for us with Jesus Christ the
Lord.

Chap. Ecclus. xxiv. — I am
the mother of fair love, and of
fear, and of knowledge, and of
holy hope.

℟. Thanks be to God.

HYMN.

HYMNUS.

VIRGO singuláris,
 Inter omnes mitis,
Nos culpis solútos,
Mites fac et castos.

 Vitam præsta puram,
Iter para tutum :
Ut vidéntes Jesum,
Semper collætémur.

 Sit laus Deo Patri,
Summo Christo decus,
Spirítui sancto,
Tribus honor unus.
 Amen.

℣. Ecce ancílla Dómini.

℟. Fiat mihi secúndum verbum tuum.
Ant. Sub tuum.

CANTICUM SIMEONIS.

Lucæ ii.

NUNC dimíttis servum tuum, Dómine,* secúndum verbum tuum, in pace ;
 Quia vidérunt óculi mei* salutáre tuum.
 Quod parásti* ante fáciem ómnium populórum ;
 Lumen ad revelatiónem Géntium ;* et glóriam plebis tuæ Israel. Gloria Patri.
 Ant. Sub tuum præsídium confúgimus, sancta Dei Génitrix : nostras deprecatiónes ne despícias in necessitátibus : sed a perículis cunctis líbera nos semper, Virgo gloriósa et benedícta.

HYMN.

Virgin of all virgins !
 To thy shelter take us :
Gentlest of the gentle !
 Chaste and gentle make us.

Still, as on we journey,
 Help our weak endeavour,
Till with thee and Jesus
 We rejoice for ever.

Through the highest heaven,
 To the Almighty Three,
Father, Son, and Spirit,
 One same glory be.
 Amen.

℣. Behold the handmaid of the Lord.

℟. Be it done unto me according to thy word.
Ant. We fly to thy patronage.

THE SONG OF SIMEON.

Luke ii.

Now dost thou dismiss thy servant, O Lord, in peace : according to thy word.
 For mine eyes have seen : thy salvation.
 Which thou hast prepared : before the face of all people.
 A light to the revealing of the gentiles : and the glory of thy people Israel. Glory, &c.
 Ant. We fly to thy patronage, O holy Mother of God : despise not our petitions in our necessities ; but deliver us always from all dangers, O glorious and blessed Virgin.

Oratio.

GRATIAM tuam, quæsumus, Domine, mentibus nostris infunde: ut qui, Angelo nuntiante, Christi Filii tui incarnationem cognovimus; per passionem ejus et crucem ad resurrectionis gloriam perducamur. Per eumdem Dominum nostrum Jesum Christum.

Ant. Virgo, &c. *ut supra ad* Laudes, *nisi* Completorium *cum Officio diei dicatur.*

TEMPORE PASCHALI.

A Vesp. Sabbati sancti usque ad Nonam Sabbati Trinit. inclusive, dicitur ut supra notatum est pro Tempore post Purificat. exceptis his quæ sequuntur.

Ad Magnificat *et ad* Benedictus.

Ant. Regína cœli, lætáre, alleluia.

Quia quem meruisti portáre, alleluia.

Resurréxit sicut dixit, alleluia.

Ora pro nobis Deum, alleluia.

Omnes aliæ Antiphonæ, Invitatoria, R͞/is post Lectiones ante V͞. et Responsiones Versiculorum terminantur cum Alleluia. *Responsoria vero Horarum dicuntur cum duobus* Alleluia.

Prayer.

Pour forth, we beseech thee, O Lord, thy grace into our hearts, that we, to whom the incarnation of Christ thy Son was made known by the message of an Angel, may, by his passion and cross, be brought to the glory of his resurrection. Through the same Christ our Lord. Amen.

Ant. O Virgin Mary, &c. *as at* Lauds, *unless* Compline *is said with the Office of the day.*

PASCHAL TIME.

From Vespers of Holy Saturday to None of Trin. Sunday inclusive, all is said as above, except what follows.

At Magnificat *and* Benedictus.

Ant. Queen of heaven, rejoice, alleluia.

For he whom thou wast meet to bear, alleluia.

Hath arisen, as he said, alleluia.

Pray to God for us, alleluia.

All the other Ants., Invits., R͞/s. after Lessons and before the V͞s., and the R͞/s. of all Versicles, are terminated with Alleluia. But the R͞/s. of the small hours (Prime, Terce, Sext, None) are said with two Alleluias.

In fine omnium Hymnorum, exceptis Hymnis de Vesp. et Complet. dicitur ℣.

Quæsumus Auctor ómnium,
In hoc Paschåli gaúdio,
Ab omni mortis ímpetu
Tuum defénde pópulum.

Glória tibi, Dómine, &c.,
as at Prime, p. 36.

Sed illi, qui ex devotione recitaverint Offic. parvum B.M.V. a I. Vesp. Ascens. usque ad Nonam Sabb. Pentecost. inclusive dicant ℣.

Tu esto nostrum gaúdium,
Qui es futúrum præmium,
Sit nostra in te glória,
Per cuncta semper sæcula.

Gloria tibi, Domine, &c.

Et a Pentec. usque ad Trinitat. dicant ℣.

Dudum sacráta péctora
Tua replésti grátia:
Dímitte nostra crímina,
Et da quiéta témpora.

Gloria tibi, Domine, &c.

Offic. Parv. B.M.V. a Vesp. Sabbati ante Dominicam primam Advent. usque ad Nonam Vigíliæ Nativit. Domini inclusive, et in die Annuntiat. dicitur ut supra notatum est pro tempore post Purific. exceptis his, quæ sequuntur.

At the end of each Hymn, except that of Vespers and Compline, is said before the last verse:

Author of all, to these our prayers,
In this glad Paschal time, attend, [snares
And from the Tempter's deadly
The people of thy choice defend.

O Jesu! born of Virgin bright,
&c., *as at* Prime, p. 36.

But those who, out of devotion, recite the little Office from first Vesp. of the Ascension to None of Pentecost Saturday, inclusive, say:

Jesu, our only joy be thou, [be;
As thou our blest reward wilt
Jesu, be thou our glory now,
And through a long eternity.

O Jesu, &c.

And from Pentecost to Trinity they say:

Thou who in ages past didst pour
Thy grace upon us from above,
That grace in us, where lost, restore, [love.
And grant us days of peace and

O Jesu, &c.

The Office of the B. V. Mary, from Vespers of the Satu day before the first Sunday of Advent to None of the Vigil of the Nativity of our Lord inclusive, and on the Feast of the Annunciation, is said as prescribed above for the season after the Purification, except what follows.

AD VESPERAS.

Ant. Prophétæ prædica-
vérunt nasci Salvatórem de
vírgine María.

Cap. Is. vii.—Ecce virgo
concipiet, et pariet fílium, et
vocabitur nomen ejus Em-
manuel. Butyrum et mel
comedet, ut sciat reprobare
malum, et eligere bonum.

Deo gratias.

Hymnus.

Ave Maris stella.
℣. Ora pro nobis.
Ad Magnificat.

Ant. Ave María, grátia
plena; Dóminus tecum:
Benedícta tu in muliéribus.
Alleluia.

Oratio.

DEUS, qui de beatæ Mariæ
Virginis utero, Verbum
tuum, Angelo nuntiante,
carnem suscipere voluisti:
præsta supplicibus tuis, ut
qui vere eam Genitricem Dei
credimus, ejus apud te in-
tercessionibus adjuvemur.
Per eumdem Dominum.

*Ad Matutinum, ante pri-
mam Lectionem dicitur:*

℣. Jube domne benedi-
cere.

Benedictio.

Alma Virgo virginum in-

AT VESPERS.

Ant. The prophets have foretold that the Saviour should be
born of the Virgin Mary.

Chap. Isaiah vii.—Behold, a
Virgin shall conceive and bear
a son, and his name shall be
called Emmanuel: butter and
honey shall he eat, that he may
know to refuse the evil, and to
choose the good.

℞. Thanks be to God.

Hymn.

Ave Maris.
℣. Pray for us, &c.
At Magnificat.

Ant. Hail Mary, full of grace;
the Lord is with thee: blessed art
thou among women.
Alleluia.

Prayer.

O God, who wast pleased that
thy Word, at the message of the
Angel, should take flesh in the
womb of the blessed Virgin
Mary; grant to us, thy suppliants, that, as we believe her
to be truly the Mother of God,
so we may be assisted by her in-
tercessions with thee. Through
the same Jesus Christ our Lord.

*At Matins, before the first
Lesson.*

℣. Pray, sir, a blessing.

The Blessing.

May the gracious Virgin of

tercédat pro nobis ad Dó-
minum. ℟. Amen.

LECTIO I. *Lucæ* i.

MISSUS est Angelus Gá-
briel a Deo in civitá-
tem Galilææ, cui nomen
Názareth, ad Vírginem de-
sponsátam viro, cui nomen
erat Joseph, de domo David,
et nomen Vírginis María.
Et ingréssus Angelus ad
eam dixit: Ave grátia plena, Dóminus tecum; bene-
dícta tu in muliéribus. Tu
autem, Domine, miserere
nostri.

℟. Deo grátias.

℟. Missus est Gábriel An-
gelus ad Maríam Vírginem
desponsátam Joseph, nún-
tians ei verbum; et expa-
véscit Virgo de lúmine: Ne
tímeas, María; invenísti
grátiam apud Dóminum.
*Ecce concípies, et páries;
et vocábitur Altíssimi Fílius.

℣. Dabit ei Dóminus De-
us sedem David patris ejus,
et regnábit in domo Jacob
in ætérnum. *Ecce concí-
pies.

℣. Jube, domne, bene-
dícere.

Benedictio.

Nos cum prole pia bene-
dícat Virgo María.
℟. Amen.

virgins intercede for us with the
Lord. ℟. Amen.

LESSON I. *Luke* i.

The Angel Gabriel was sent by
God to a city of Galilee, called
Nazareth, to a Virgin espoused
to a man whose name was Joseph, of the house of David:
and the virgin's name was Mary:
and the Angel having entered,
said unto her: Hail, full of grace,
the Lord is with thee; blessed
art thou among women. But
thou, O Lord, have mercy on us.

℟. Thanks be to God.

℟. The Angel Gabriel was
sent to the Virgin Mary, espoused to Joseph, to announce
to her the divine message: but
the light of his countenance af-
frighted the sacred Virgin. Do
not fear, Mary; thou hast found
grace with the Lord. Behold,
thou shalt conceive, and bring
forth one who shall be called the
Son of the Most High.

℣. The Lord God shall give
him the throne of his father
David, and he shall reign over
the house of Jacob for ever.*
Behold.

℣. Pray, sir, a blessing.

The Blessing.

May the Virgin Mary, with
her loving Son, bless us.
℟. Amen.

QUÆ cum audísset, turbáta est in sermóne ejus, et cogitábat qualis esset ista salutátio. Et ait Angelus ei: Ne tímeas, María; invenísti enim grátiam apud Deum. Ecce concípies in útero, et paries filium, et vocábis nomen ejus Jesum. Hic erit magnus, et Fílius Altíssimi vocábitur. Et dabit illi Dóminus Deus sedem David patris ejus, et regnábit in domo Jacob in ætérnum; et regni ejus non erit finis. Tu autem, Domine, miserere nostri.

R̶. Deo grátias.

R̶. Ave María, grátia plena, Dóminus tecum. * Spíritus Sanctus supervéniet in te, et virtus Altíssimi obumbrábit tibi : quod enim ex te nascétur sanctum, vocábitur Fílius Dei.

V̶. Quómodo fiet istud, quóniam virum non cognósco? Et respóndens Angelus dixit ei: *Spiritus Sanctus supervéniet, &c.

V̶. Jube, domne, &c.

Benedictio.

Sancta Dei Genitrix sit nobis auxiliátrix.

R̶. Amen.

Mary having heard these words was much troubled, and reflected on what kind of salutation this could be. And the Angel said to her : Do not fear, Mary, for thou hast found grace with God : behold, thou shalt conceive in thy womb, and shalt bring forth a Son, and shalt call his name Jesus. He shall be great, and shall be called the Son of the Most High : the Lord God will give him the throne of his father David, and he shall reign over the house of Jacob for ever, and of his kingdom there shall be no end. But thou, O Lord, have mercy on us.

R̶. Thanks be to God.

R̶. Hail Mary, full of grace, the Lord is with thee. The Holy Ghost shall descend upon thee, and the power of the Most High shall overshadow thee: for the Holy One who shall be born of thee shall be called the Son of God.

V̶. How shall this be done, because I know not man ? The Angel answering, said to her: * The Holy Ghost shall descend upon thee, &c.

V̶. Pray, sir, a blessing.

The Blessing.

May the holy Mother of God be our helper.

R̶. Amen.

LECTIO III.

DIXIT autem María ad Angelum: Quómodo fiet istud, quóniam virum non cognósco? Et respóndens Angelus dixit ei: Spíritus Sanctus supervéniet in te, et virtus Altíssimi obumbrábit tibi. Ideóque et quod nascétur ex te sanctum, vocábitur Fílius Dei. Et ecce Elísabeth, cognáta tua, et ipsa concépit fílium in senectúte sua. Et hic mensis sextus est illi, quæ vocátur stérilis; quia non erit impossibile apud Deum omne verbum. Dixit autem María: Ecce ancílla Dómini, fiat mihi secúndum verbum tuum. Tu autem, Domine, miserere nostri.

℟. Deo grátias.

℟. Súscipe verbum, Virgo María, quod tibi a Dómino per Angelum transmíssum est: concípies, et páries Deum páriter et hóminem. * Ut benedícta dicáris inter omnes mulíeres.

℣. Páries quidem fílium et virginitátis non patiéris detriméntum: efficiéris grávida, et eris mater semper intácta. * Ut benedícta dicáris inter omnes mulíeres.

Glória Patri.

LESSON III.

Then Mary said to the Angel: How shall this be done, for I know not man? The Angel answered her: The Holy Ghost shall descend upon thee, and the power of the Most High shall overshadow thee: therefore the Holy One who shall be born of thee shall be called the Son of God. And behold, thy cousin Elizabeth hath conceived a son in her old age; and this month is the sixth to her, who is called barren: for with God nothing shall be impossible. Mary then replied: Behold the handmaid of the Lord, be it done to me according to thy word. But thou, O Lord, have mercy on us.

℟. Thanks be to God.

℟. Receive, O Virgin Mary, the word which the Lord declared to thee by the ministry of the Angel: thou shalt conceive, and bring forth a Son, who will be both God and Man. * That thou mayest be called blessed among all women.

℣. Thou shalt bring forth a Son, and shalt suffer no detriment to thy virginity: thou shalt become a mother without ceasing to be a chaste virgin. * That thou mayest be called blessed among all women.

Glory, &c.

* Ut benedícta dicáris inter omnes mulíeres.

Súscipe, &c.

AD LAUDES.

Ant. Prophétæ prædicavérunt nasci Salvatórem de Vírgine María.

Cap. Isaiæ xi.—Egrediétur virga de radíce Jesse, et flos de radíce ejus ascéndet. Et requiéscet super eum Spíritus Dómini.

R̶̷. Deo grátias.

Ad Benedictus.

Ant. Spíritus sanctus in te descéndet María, ne tímeas: habébis in útero Fílium Dei. Alleluia.

Oratio.

DEUS, qui de beatæ, &c., *ut supra*, p. 64.

AD PRIMAM.

Ant. Prophétæ prædicavérunt nasci Salvatórem de Vírgine María.

Cap. Isaiæ xlv.—Roráte cœli désuper, et nubes pluant justum: aperiátur terra, et gérminet Salvatórem: et justítia oriátur simul: ego Dóminus creávi eum.

R̶̷. Deo grátias.

Oratio.

DEUS, qui de beatæ, &c.

R̶̷. That thou mayest be called blessed among all women.

Receive, O Virgin Mary, &c. *to the V.*

AT LAUDS.

Ant. The prophets have foretold that the Redeemer should be born of the Virgin Mary.

Chap. Isai. xi.—There shall spring forth a branch out of the root of Jesse, and a flower shall arise out of its stock: and the Spirit of the Lord shall rest upon him.

R̶̷. Thanks be to God.

The Hymn (*as above*).

At Benedictus.

Ant. The Holy Ghost shall descend upon thee, Mary: fear not, thou shalt bear in thy womb the Son of God. Alleluia.

Prayer.

O God, who wast pleased, &c. (*as above at Vespers*), p. 64.

AT PRIME.

Ant. (*as at Lauds*). The Prophets have, &c.

Chap. Isai. xlv.—Drop down dew, ye heavens, from above, and let the clouds rain the just: let the earth be opened, and bud forth the Saviour; and let justice spring up together; I the Lord have created him.

R̶̷. Thanks be to God.

Prayer (*as above*).

AD TERTIAM.

Ant. AngelusDómini nuntiávit Maríæ, et concépit de Spíritu sancto.

Cap. Ecce virgo concípiát, et páriet fílium, et vocábitur nomen ejus Emmánuel. Bútyrum et mel cómedet, ut sciat reprobáre malum, et elígere bonum.

℟. Deo grátias.

Oratio.

DEUS, qui de beatæ, &c.

AT TERCE.

Ant. The Angel of the Lord announced unto Mary, and she conceived of the Holy Ghost.

Chap. Isai. vii. — Behold, a virgin shall conceive, and bring forth a Son, and his name shall be called Emmanuel. He shall eat butter and honey, that he may know how to reject evil and choose good.

℟. Thanks be to God.

Prayer (*as above*).

AD SEXTAM.

Ant. Oriétur sicut sol Salvátor mundi : et descéndet in úterum Vírginis, sicut imber super gramen.

Cap. Egredietur, &c., *ut supra in* Laudibus.

Oratio.

DEUS, qui de beatæ, &c.

AT SEXT.

Ant. The Saviour of the world shall arise like the sun, and shall descend into the womb of a Virgin, as a shower of rain upon grass.

Chap. Isai. xi. (*as at Lauds*).

Prayer (*as above*).

AD NONAM.

Ant. María autem conservábat ómnia verba hæc, cónferens in corde suo.

Cap. Luc. i.—Dabit illi Dóminus Deus sedem David patris ejus : et regnábit in domo Jacob in æternum, et regni ejus non erit finis.

℟. Deo grátias.

Oratio.

DEUS, qui de beatæ, &c.

AT NONE.

Ant. But Mary kept all these words, pondering them in her heart.

Chap. Luke i.—The Lord God will give him the throne of his father David, and he shall reign over the house of Jacob for ever, and of his kingdom there shall be no end.

℟. Thanks be to God.

Prayer (*as above*).

A Nativitate usque ad Octavum Purificationis beatæ Virginis inclusive, Officium dicitur, ut supra notatum est pro tempore post Purificationem, exceptis his quæ sequuntur.

From the Nativity to the Octave of the Purification, inclusive, the Office is said as in the season of the Purification, except what follows.

AD VESPERAS.

Ant. O admirábile commércium! Creátor géneris humáni animátum corpus súmens, de Vírgine nasci dignátus est: et procédens homo sine sémine, largítus est nobis suam Deitátem.

Ad Magnificat.

Ant. Nésciens mater Virgo virum péperit sine dolóre Salvatórem sæculórum: ipsum Regem Angelórum sola Virgo lactábat úbere de cœlo pleno.

AT VESPERS.

Ant. O wonderful intercourse! the Creator of mankind, assuming a body animated with a soul, was pleased to be born of a Virgin; and becoming man without human concurrence, he made us partakers of his divine nature.

At Magnificat.

Ant. The Virgin Mother not knowing man, brought forth the Saviour of the world without pain; she alone a pure Virgin, nourished him, the King of Angels, with her breast filled from heaven.

Oratio.

DEUS, qui salútis ætérnæ, beátæ Maríæ virginitáte fecúnda, humáno géneri præmia præstátisti; tríbue quæsumus, ut ipsam pro nobis intercédere sentiámus, per quam merúimus auctórem vitæ suscípere Dóminum nostrum Jesum Christum Filium tuum: Qui tecum vivit et regnat in unitáte Spíritus sancti Deus per omnia sæcula sæculórum. Amen.

Quæ dicitur ad omnes horas, excepto Completorio.

Prayer.

O God, who, by the fruitful virginity of blessed Mary, hast given to mankind the rewards of eternal salvation; grant, we beseech thee, that we may experience her intercession for us, through whom we merited to receive the author of life, our Lord Jesus Christ, thy Son, who liveth and reigneth with thee and the Holy Ghost, one God, world without end. Amen.

This prayer is said at all the hours, Compline *excepted.*

AD LAUDES.

Ant. O admirábile commércium, &c. (*ut supra*, p. 70.)

Ad Benedictus.

Ant. Virgo verbum concépit, virgo permánsit. Virgo
péperit Regem·ómnium re-
gum.

Oratio.

DEUS, qui salútis ætérnæ,
&c. (*ut supra*, p. 70.)

AD PRIMAM.

Ant. O admirábile com-
mércium.

Oratio.

DEUS, qui salútis ætérnæ,
&c.

AD TERTIAM.

Ant. Quando natus es in-
effabíliter ex Vírgine, tunc
implétæ sunt Scriptúræ: sicut plúvia in vellus descen-
dísti, ut salvum fáceres ge-
nus humánum: te laudámus
Deus noster.

Oratio.

DEUS, qui salútis ætérnæ,
&c.

AD SEXTAM.

Ant. Rubum, quem ví-
derat Moyses incombústum,
conservátam agnóvimus tu-
am laudábilem virginitá-
tem: Dei Génitrix, inter-
céde pro nobis.

Oratio.

DEUS, qui salútis ætérnæ,
&c.

AT LAUDS.

Ant. O wonderful intercourse,
&c. (*as above*, p. 70.)

At Benedictus.

Ant. A Virgin conceived the
Word, and remained a virgin.
A Virgin brought forth the King
of all kings.

Prayer.

O God, who, by the fruitful,
&c. (*as above*, p. 70.)

AT PRIME.

Ant. O wonderful intercourse,
&c. (*as above*.)

Prayer (*as above*).

AT TERCE.

Ant. When thou wast born
after an ineffable manner, the
Scriptures were then fulfilled:
thou didst descend like rain upon
a fleece to save mankind: O our
God, we give thee praise.

Prayer (*as above*).

AT SEXT.

Ant. In the bush, which Moses
saw burning without consuming,
we acknowledge the preserva-
tion of thy admirable virginity:
O Mother of God, make intercession for us.

Prayer (*as above*).

AD NONAM.

Ant. Ecce Maria génuit nobis Salvatórem: quem Joánnes videns, exclamávit, dicens: Ecce Agnus Dei: ecce qui tollit peccáta mundi. Alleluia.

Oratio.

DEUS, qui salútis ætérnæ, &c.

AT NONE.

Ant. Behold, Mary hath borne us the Saviour, whom John seeing, exclaimed: Behold the Lamb of God, behold him who taketh away the sins of the world. Alleluia.

Prayer (*as above*).

SUPPLEMENT

OF

COMMEMORATIONS

Commemorations are made at Lauds
after the final prayer.

November 29

BL. DIONYSIUS AND REDEMPTUS

Ant.

FOR the kingdom of heaven   *
is theirs; who despising the life of this
world, attained to the rewards of heaven,
and washed their robes in the blood of
the Lamb.

℞. God is wonderful in his saints.

℣. And glorious in his majesty.

Let us pray: *Prayer*

O God, who in thy wondrous providence, didst lead blessed Dionysius and Redemptus through the perils of the sea to the palm of martyrdom, grant through their intercession that in the midst of earthly vicissitudes and wordly desires we may remain steadfast even unto death in the praise of thy name: through Christ our Lord.   Amen.

December 5

BL. BARTHOLOMEW FANTI

Ant.

WELL done   *   thou good and faithful servant; because thou hast been faithful over a few things I will place thee over many things, saith the Lord.

℞ The just shall spring as the lily.

℣ And flourish for ever before the Lord.

Let us pray: *Prayer*

O God, who didst make blessed Bartholomew renowned for devotion to thy Holy Eucharist and fidelity to religious observance, graciously grant that by his intercession and example, we may be detached from things of earth, cling to thee alone and love thee perfectly: who livest and reignest for ever and ever. Amen.

December 11

BL. FRANCUS

Ant.

WELL done   *   thou good and faithful servant; because thou hast been faithful over a few things I will place thee over many things, saith the Lord.

℞ The just shall spring as the lily.

℣ And flourish for ever before the Lord.

Let us pray: *Prayer*

O God, who dost manifest thine omnipotence chiefly in showing pardon and pity graciously grant, that as thou hast called the Carmelite, blessed Francus, made glorious by his merits, to the heavenly kingdom, so mayest thou, by his merits and prayers, cleanse us from the stains of our sins: through Christ our Lord.   Amen.

December 14

S. SPIRIDION

Ant.

WELL done   *   thou good and
faithful servant; because thou hast
been faithful over a few things I will
place thee over many things, saith the
Lord.

℞ The just shall spring as the lily.

℣ And flourish for ever before
the Lord.

Let us pray: *Prayer*

MAY the feast of Saint Spiridion, thy
confessor and bishop, protect us, O
Lord; and as he was, in prayer and works,
the faithful follower of the Order instituted by the prophet Elias, so may we, by
following in his footsteps, enjoy thee with
him for ever; through Christ our Lord.
Amen.

December 16

BL. MARY OF THE ANGELS

Ant.

THE kingdom of heaven   *   is
like a net that was cast into the sea,
and enclosed fish of every kind at once;

when it was full, the fishermen drew it out, and sat on the beach, where they stored all that was worth keeping in their vessels, and threw the useless kind away.

℞ God chose and predestined her.

℣ And gave her a place in his tabernacle.

Let us pray: *Prayer*

O God, who hast made the blessed Mary, thy virgin, to live like an angel: grant to us thy servants that, following in her footsteps, we may overcome the desires of the flesh and be worthy to enjoy the companionship of the angels: through Christ our Lord.   Amen.

December 30

S. DIONYSIUS

Ant.

WELL done   *   thou good and faithful servant; because thou hast been faithful over a few things I will place thee over many things, saith the Lord.

℞ The just shall spring as the lily.

℣ And flourish for ever before the Lord.

Let us pray: *Prayer*

MAY our vices, O Lord, we beseech thee, be healed by the remedies of thy mercy; that through the loving intercession of the blessed Dionysius, thy confessor and bishop, we may ascend to heavenly desires: through Christ our Lord.   Amen.

January 2

S. EUPHROSYNE

Ant.

THE kingdom of heaven   *   is like a net that was cast into the sea, and enclosed fish of every kind at once; when it was full, the fishermen drew it out, and sat on the beach, where they stored all that was worth keeping in their vessels, and threw the useless kind away.

℞ God chose and predestined her.

℣ And gave her a place in his tabernacle.

Let us pray: *Prayer*

O God, who didst marvellously incite thy holy virgin Euphrosyne to the pursuit of holiness and didst always guide her in its path, do thou through her merits and intercession make us burn with perfect love: through Christ our Lord. Amen.

January 16

S. PETER THOMAS

Ant.

A grain of wheat   *   must fall into the ground and die, or else it remains nothing more than a grain of wheat; but if it dies, then it yields rich fruit.

℞ Great is his glory in thy salvation.

℣ Thou hast crowned him with honour and beauty.

Let us pray: *Prayer*

BE thou appeased, we beseech thee, Lord, by the merits and intercession of thy blessed martyr-bishop Saint Peter Thomas; grant us the pardon of our sins, and preserve us from the evils of pestilence: through Christ our Lord. Amen.

January 19

S. TELESPHORUS

Ant.

A grain of wheat   *   must fall into the ground and die, or else it remains nothing more than a grain of wheat; but if it dies, then it yields rich fruit.

℞ Great is his glory in thy salvation.

℣. Thou hast crowned him with honour and beauty.

Let us pray: *Prayer*

O God, who didst call Saint Telesphorus from the desert to the supreme government of thy Church and to the triumph of martyrdom; grant, we beseech thee, that, bearing all trials with a humble heart for the glory of thy name, we may obtain the palm of heavenly glory: through Christ our Lord.   Amen.

January 22

S. ANASTASIUS

Ant.

A grain of wheat   *   must fall into the ground and die, or else it remains nothing more than a grain of wheat; but if it dies, then it yields rich fruit.

℞ Great is his glory in thy salvation.

℣. Thou hast crowned him with honour and beauty.

Let us pray: *Prayer*

O God, strength of those who hope in thee, who didst call blessed Anastasius from the solitude of Carmel to the palm of martyrdom: we beseech thee that, animated by his example, we may endure our salutary trials in patience: through Christ our Lord.　　Amen.

January 28

BL. ARCHANGELA

Ant.

THE kingdom of heaven　　*　　is like a net that was cast into the sea, and enclosed fish of every kind at once; when it was full, the fishermen drew it out, and sat on the beach, where they stored all that was worth keeping in their vessels, and threw the useless kind away.

℞ God chose and predestined her.

℣ And gave her a place in his tabernacle.

Let us pray: *Prayer*

O God, who hast specially favoured the virgin, blessed Archangela, from her youth in preparation for thy gift of heroic virtue: grant through her intercession, that having been protected by the gift of thy grace upon earth we may deserve to join the choirs of the blessed in heaven: through Christ our Lord. Amen.

February 4

S. ANDREW CORSINI

Ant.

HE did what was right * in the sight of the Lord, and the Lord directed him in all things, helped him and revealed his name to him.

℟ The just shall spring as the lily.

℣ And flourish for ever before the Lord.

Let us pray: *Prayer*

O God, who art ever fashioning new models of virtue in thy Church, grant that thy people may so follow in the footsteps of thy confessor and bishop blessed Andrew, as to obtain a like reward: through Christ our Lord. Amen.

February 9

S. CYRIL OF ALEXANDRIA

Ant.

WELL done * thou good and faithful servant; because thou hast been faithful over a few things I will place thee over many things, saith the Lord.

℟ The just shall spring as the lily.

℣ And flourish for ever before the Lord.

Let us pray: *Prayer*

FATHER of celestial light, who didst deign to fill with the light of true faith and wisdom the mind of thy blessed confessor and bishop, Cyril, so that he might save the honour of the Mother of thy Son, the ever-virgin Mary, from being tarnished by error; grant through his intercession that the hearts of the erring may return to the unity of thy truth and that we may find concord in thy will: through the same Christ our Lord. Amen.

February 25 (in leap-year 26)

S. AVERTANUS

Ant.

WELL done   *   thou good and faithful servant; because thou hast been faithful over a few things I will place thee over many things, saith the Lord.

℞ The just shall spring as the lily.

℣ And flourish for ever before the Lord.

Let us pray: *Prayer*

GRANT, we beseech thee, O Lord, that we may perfectly imitate the religious life of thy blessed confessor, Avertanus, under the banner of thy Mother, Mary of Mt. Carmel, and through his intercession be strengthened in every virtue: who livest and reignest for ever and ever. Amen.

March 3

BL. JACOBINUS

Ant.

WELL done   *   thou good and faithful servant; because thou hast been faithful over a few things I will place thee over many things, saith the Lord.

℞ The just shall spring as the lily.

℣ And flourish for ever before the Lord.

Let us pray: *Prayer*

POUR out upon us, we beseech thee, O Lord, through the intercession of thy blessed confessor Jacobinus, the spirit of penance and prayer, so that, following his glorious example, we may reach eternal glory: through Christ our Lord. Amen.

March 4

BL. ROMAEUS

Ant.

WELL done   *   thou good and faithful servant; because thou hast been faithful over a few things I will place thee over many things, saith the Lord.

℟ The just shall spring as the lily.

℣ And flourish for ever before the Lord.

Let us pray: *Prayer*

O God, who didst lead blessed Romaeus along the paths of justice in his pilgrimage with thy servant Avertanus, grant that we may be fortified by the help of his intercession and be led to our heavenly home: through Christ our Lord. Amen.

March 6

S. CYRIL OF CONSTANTINOPLE·

Ant.

WELL done * thou good and faithful servant; because thou hast been faithful over a few things I will place thee over many things, saith the Lord.

℞ The just shall spring as the lily.

℣. And flourish for ever before the Lord.

Let us pray: *Prayer*

O God, who by the apparition of an angel didst reveal future events to thy blessed Doctor, Cyril, while he offered Mass on Mt. Carmel, grant that following him we may be detached from earthly things and ever seek the eternal: through Christ our Lord.   Amen.

March 11

S. TERESA MARGARET REDI

Ant.

THE kingdom of heaven * is like a net that was cast into the sea, and enclosed fish of every kind at once; when it was full, the fishermen drew it out, and sat on the beach, where they stored all that was worth keeping in their vessels, and threw the useless kind away.

℟. God chose and predestined her.

℣. And gave her a place in his tabernacle.

Let us pray: *Prayer*

O God, who didst grant to the virgin, blessed Teresa Margaret, to draw from the wounds of our Saviour the priceless treasures of purity and love, grant to us also that through her intercession we may abound in these same heavenly gifts: through the same Christ our Lord.   Amen.

March 13

S. EUPHRASIA

Ant.

THE kingdom of heaven   *   is like a net that was cast into the sea, and enclosed fish of every kind at once; when it was full, the fishermen drew it out, and sat on the beach, where they stored all that was worth keeping in their vessels, and threw the useless kind away.

℟. God chose and predestined her.

℣. And gave her a place in his tabernacle.

Let us pray   *Prayer*

O God, who makest the Church ever fruitful with new offspring, give ear unto thy suppliants, that, as thou hast adorned the holy virgin Euphrasia with virtues and miracles, we may be delivered through her intercession from the darkness of vice: through Christ our Lord. Amen.

March 19

S. JOSEPH

Ant.

BEHOLD the faithful and prudent servant   *   whom the Lord placed over his family.

℞. Glory and riches are in his house.

℣. And justice remains forever.

Let us pray   *Prayer*

O God, who in thy ineffable providence didst choose S. Joseph to be the spouse of thy most holy Mother, grant that we may have him for our intercessor in heaven whom we venerate as our protector on earth: thou who art God, living and reigning with God the Father, in the unity of the Holy Spirit, for ever and ever. Amen.

March 20

BL. BAPTIST OF MANTUA

Ant.

WELL done   *   thou good and faithful servant; because thou hast been faithful over a few things I will place thee over many things, saith the Lord.

℞ The just shall spring as the lily.

℣ And flourish as ever before the Lord.

Let us pray   *Prayer*

O God, who hast made thy blessed Confessor Baptist illustrious in his contempt for the world and in his zeal for thy glory, give us the strength to renounce worldly vanities and to seek with an upright mind the things that are thine: through Christ our Lord.   Amen.

March 24

S. GABRIEL, PROTECTOR OF ORDER

Ant.

THE angel Gabriel   *   came down to Zachary and said to him: thy wife is to bear thee a son and you will call his name John and many will rejoice in his birth: he will go before the face of the Lord to prepare his ways. *PT* Alleluia.

℞ Adore the Lord.

℣ All his angels. *PT* Alleluia.

Let us pray *Prayer*

O God, who from the angelic ranks didst choose the archangel Gabriel to herald the mystery of thy incarnation, grant us this favour, that we who keep his feast on earth may feel the power of his advocacy in heaven: thou who livest and reignest for ever and ever. Amen.

March 29

S. BERTHOLD

Ant.

WELL done * thou good and faithful servant; because thou hast been faithful over a few things I will place thee over many things, saith the Lord. *PT* Alleluia.

℞ The just shall spring as the lily.

℣ And flourish for ever before the Lord. *PT* Alleluia.

Let us pray   *Prayer*

MAY the venerable feast of thy blessed confessor Berthold guard us, Lord, and may we experience the unceasing protection of him who so virtuously governed and spread the Order of Carmel: through Christ our Lord.   Amen.

March 31

BL. JOAN OF TOULOUSE

Ant.

THE kingdom of heaven   *   is like a net that was cast into the sea, and enclosed fish of every kind at once; when it was full, the fishermen drew it out, and sat on the beach, where they stored all that was worth keeping in their vessels, and threw the useless kind away. *PT* Alleluia.

℞. God chose and predestined her.

℣. And gave her a place in his tabernacle. *PT* Alleluia.

Let us pray   *Prayer*

O God, who in thy blessed virgin Joan has shown us a wonderful model of penance and charity, grant, we beseech thee, that faithfully imitating her example

we may successfully attain the reward
thou hast promised to those who love
thee: through Christ our Lord.
Amen.

April 18

BL. MARY OF THE INCARNATION

Ant.

THE kingdom of heaven   *   is
like a net that was cast into the sea,
and enclosed fish of every kind at once;
when it was full, the fishermen drew it
out, and sat on the beach, where they
stored all that was worth keeping in their
vessels, and threw the useless kind away.
PT Alleluia.

℟ God chose and predestined her.

℣ And gave her a place in his
tabernacle. *PT* Alleluia.

Let us pray   *Prayer*

O God, the giver of all good gifts, who
didst strengthen blessed Mary with
burning zeal for thy glory, and with
wonderful fortitude in adversity, through
her merits enable thy servants to bear all
trials bravely, and persevere in the love
of thy holy religion: through Christ our
Lord.   Amen.

May 5

S. ANGELUS

Ant.

BLESSED Angelus,   *   who didst restore speech to the dumb, hearing to the deaf, sight to the blind and call the dead to life, aid those who sit in darkness and in the shadow of death, alleluia.

℞ Precious in the sight of the Lord.

℣ Is the death of his saints, alleluia.

Let us pray   *Prayer*

LET thy people glorify thee, O Lord, by honouring thy blessed priest and martyr Angelus, and through his intercession, may they deserve to be guided by thee: through Christ our Lord. Amen.

May 11

BL. ALOYSIUS RABATA

Ant.

WELL done   *   thou good and faithful servant; because thou hast been faithful over a few things I will place thee over many things, saith the Lord, alleluia.

℞ The just shall spring as the lily.

℣ And flourish for ever before the Lord, alleluia.

Let us pray: *Prayer*

O God, who didst adorn the blessed Aloysius with extraordinary charity and with patience in bearing injuries, grant that, by imitating him whose feast we celebrate in the practice of charity and in the love of our enemies, we may deserve an eternal reward: through Christ our Lord.   Amen.

May 16

S. SIMON STOCK

Ant.

BLESSED Simon   *   shone in his day as the morning star; like the sun, he brightened the sanctuary of God and the memory of him is the blessing of his posterity, alleluia.

℞ The just shall spring as the lily.

℣ And flourish for ever before the Lord, alleluia.

Let us pray: *Prayer*

O God, who by the merits and prayers of thy confessor Simon didst so singularly honour the Order of Mount Carmel at the hands of the Mother of thy Son, our Lord, Jesus Christ, grant that through his intercession we may attain to the glory thou hast prepared for those who love thee: through the same Christ our Lord.   Amen.

May 22
S. JOACHIMA DE VEDRUNA

Ant.

THE kingdom of heaven   *   is like a net that was cast into the sea, and enclosed fish of every kind at once; when it was full, the fishermen drew it out, and sat on the beach, where they stored all that was worth keeping in their vessels, and threw the useless kind away. *PT* Alleluia.

℟ God chose and predestined her.

℣ And gave her a place in his tabernacle. *PT* Alleluia.

Let us pray: *Prayer*

GOD, who for the christian education of youth and the solace of the sick, didst, through blessed Joachima, form a new family in the Church; grant, we beseech thee, that as we rejoice in her merits we may profit by the example of

such virtue: through Christ our Lord.
Amen.

May 25

S. MARY MAGDALENE DE PAZZI

Ant.

MARY Magdalene,   *   the virgin, chose the better part which shall not be taken from her; most pure in life, she remained incorrupt even after her death. *PT* Alleluia.

℞ God chose and predestined her.

℣ And gave her a place in his tabernacle. *PT* Alleluia.

Let us pray: *Prayer*

GOD, who lovest virginity and didst inflame the blessed maiden Mary Magdalene with love of thee, adorning her with heavenly gifts, grant that we who keep this festival in her honour may emulate her purity and charity: through Christ our Lord.   Amen.

June 7

BL. ANNE OF S. BARTHOLOMEW

Ant.

THE kingdom of heaven   *   is like a net that was cast into the sea,

and enclosed fish of every kind at once;
when it was full, the fishermen drew it
out, and sat on the beach, where they
stored all that was worth keeping in their
vessels, and threw the useless kind away.
PT Alleluia.

℞ God chose and predestined her.

℣ And gave her a place in his
tabernacle. *PT* Alleluia.

L. Let us pray: *Prayer*

GOD, who didst mould blessed Anne,
thy virgin, into a singular model of
humility, grant to us thy servants that,
following in her footsteps, we may be
worthy to receive the reward promised to
the humble: through Christ our Lord.
Amen.

June 14

S. ELISEUS

Ant.

WHEN the sons of the prophet
* from Jerico that stood
watching saw him, they said: the spirit
of Elias has come down to rest on
Eliseus; and so, meeting him, they fell
down face to earth. *PT* Alleluia.

℞ Eliseus did great things in his lifetime.

℣ And even after death he worked miracles. *PT* Alleluia.

Let us pray: *Prayer*

ALMIGHTY and eternal God, whose glories were marvellously proclaimed by thy chosen prophets, grant, we beseech thee, that even as thou didst give the double spirit of Elias to thy prophet Eliseus, so thou wilt deign to increase within us thy grace of the Holy Spirit to enable us to perform virtuous deeds: through Christ our Lord.   Amen.

July 9

BL. JOAN SCOPELLI

Ant.

THE kingdom of heaven   *   is like a net that was cast into the sea, and enclosed fish of every kind at once; when it was full, the fishermen drew it out, and sat on the beach, where they stored all that was worth keeping in their vessels, and threw the useless kind away.

℞ God chose and predestined her.

℣ And gave her a place in his tabernacle.

Let us pray:　　　　　　*Prayer*

O God, help of those who cry to thee, who didst strengthen blessed Joan with the spirit of prayer and penance against the wiles of the demon; by her merits and intercession strengthen us with a like spirit, so that we may withstand the attacks of the enemy and gain the palm of victory: through Christ our Lord. Amen.

July 20

S. ELIAS,
PROPHET, FATHER OF OUR ORDER

Ant.

E LIAS was a man　　　*　　　like ourselves, subject to the same infirmities; and he prayed earnestly that it might not rain upon the earth, and it did not rain for three years and six months. He prayed again, and the heavens gave rain, and the earth brought forth its fruit.

℟ By the word of the Lord he shut up the heavens.

℣ And he brought down fire from heaven thrice.

Let us pray:　　　　　　*Prayer*

G RANT, we beseech thee, Almighty God, that as thou didst lift up our holy father, thy prophet Elias, in a fiery chariot into heaven before he might die according to nature: so also may we through his intercession be lifted above the things of earth during our mortal life, and rejoice with him in the resurrection of the just: through our Lord Jesus Christ, thy Son, who is God, living and reigning with thee, in the unity of the Holy Spirit, for ever and ever. Amen.

July 24

BL. TERESA OF S. AUGUSTINE AND COMPANIONS

Ant.

THESE are the prudent virgins   * who, having provided themselves with oil, went out to bring the bridegroom and his bride home; and having met him, they escorted him to the wedding.

℞. O prudent virgins.

℣. Make ready your lamps.

Let us pray: *Prayer*

O God, who for their unshaken constancy in thy love didst call blessed Teresa and her companions from the summit of Carmel to the crown of martyrdom, grant, we beseech thee, that loving thee faithfully, we may be brought to the contemplation of the grandeur of thy majesty: who livest and reignest for ever and ever.   Amen.

July 26

S. ANNE

Ant.

A NNE,   *   noble women, reigning for ever with the angels, be mindful of us that we, too, may merit to be with them.

℞. God chose and predestined her.

℣. And gave her a place in his tabernacle.

Let us pray: *Prayer*

O God, who didst deign to bestow such grace on blessed Anne that she was worthy to bear in her womb blessed Mary thy Mother, grant us, through the intercession of both mother and child, the abundance of thy mercy; that as we devoutly and lovingly esteem their memory, we may, through their prayers, be worthy to come to the heavenly Jerusalem: who livest and reignest for ever and ever. Amen.

July 28

BL. JOHN SORETH

Ant.

WELL done   *   thou good and faithful servant; because thou hast been faithful over a few things I will place thee over many things, saith the Lord.

℟ The just shall spring as the lily.

℣ And flourish for ever before the Lord.

Let us pray: *Prayer*

O God, the dispenser of all good gifts, who didst endow blessed John with a burning zeal for thy honour and with extraordinary courage in confronting dangers, grant us through his merits and prayers to bear all our trials and to persevere in thy love: through Christ our Lord.   Amen.

August 7

S. ALBERT OF SICILY

Ant.

MAY the heavenly servant   *   of Christ, Albert, favourably direct our footsteps; may he instruct us well in the way of peace, be a light to Christ's faithful, offer fitting prayers to Christ for us and enrich us with his own shining virtues.

℞ The just shall spring as the lily.

℣ And flourish for ever before the Lord.

Let us pray: *Prayer*

O God, who didst deign to call the blessed confessor Albert to forsake the world and to embrace the Order of thy dear Mother Mary, grant, we pray thee, that through his merits and example we may serve thee worthily and with him enjoy thee for ever in eternal glory: thou who livest and reignest for ever and ever. Amen.

August 16

S. JOACHIM

Ant.

LET us praise   *   a man who was famous in his own generation, for God gave him the blessing of all nations, and confirmed his covenant upon his head.

℞ His seed shall be mighty upon the earth.

℣. The generation of the righteous shall be blessed.

Let us pray: *Prayer*

GOD, who out of all thy saints didst choose blessed Joachim to be the father of her who bore thy Son, grant, we pray thee, that we who pay honour to his festival may feel the power of his unfailing protection: through Christ our Lord.   Amen.

August 17

BL. ANGELUS AUGUSTINE MAZZINGHI

Ant.

WELL done   *   thou good and faithful servant; because thou hast been faithful over a few things I will place thee over many things, saith the Lord.

℞. The just shall spring as the lily.

℣. And flourish for ever before the Lord.

Let us pray: *Prayer*

O God, who dost gladden us with the yearly festival of thy blessed confessor Angelus, grant that since he has been a champion of the religious life on earth, we may deserve to have him as our glorious patron in heaven: through Christ our Lord. Amen.

August 27

THE WOUNDING OF THE HEART OF S. TERESA

Ant.

THE Lord * set me up as a sign; he surrounded me with his spears and drained my life away.

℞. Thy arrows are fixed in me.

℣. And thou hast laid thy hand securely upon me.

Let us pray: *Prayer*

O God, who didst transfix with a burning dart the unsullied heart of the holy virgin Teresa, thy spouse, and didst consecrate her as a victim of love, grant by her intercession that our hearts may burn with the flame of the Holy Spirit and may love thee in all and above all: who livest and reignest for ever and ever. Amen.

September 2

S. BROCARD

Ant.

WELL done   *   thou good and faithful servant; because thou hast been faithful over a few things I will place thee over many things, saith the Lord.

℟ The just shall spring as the lily.

℣ And flourish for ever before the Lord.

Let us pray: *Prayer*

SANCTIFY thy servants, Lord, who humbly beseech thee on the feast of blessed Brocard, hermit of Mount Carmel and thy confessor, that by his salutary patronage our life may be everywhere protected in adversity: through Christ our Lord.   Amen.

September 16

S. ALBERT,
THE LAWGIVER OF THE ORDER

Ant.

WELL done   *   thou good and faithful servant; because thou hast been faithful over a few things I will place thee over many things, saith the Lord.

℞ The just shall spring as the lily.

℣ And flourish for ever before the Lord.

Let us pray: *Prayer*

M AY the fulness of thy blessing descend upon us abundantly, Lord, and be thou ever appeased by the intercession of blessed Albert, thy confessor and bishop: through Christ our Lord. Amen.

September 26

S. GERARD

Ant.

A grain of wheat   *   must fall into the ground and die, or else it remains nothing more than a grain of wheat; but if it dies, then it yields rich fruit.

℞ Great is his glory in thy salvation.

℣ Thou hast crowned him with honour and beauty.

Let us pray: *Prayer*

WE dedicate unto thee, O Lord, this sacred day on which the blessed Gerard was cast headlong from the summit of a mountain by the enemies of thy name, beseeching thy clemency, that the holy sufferings of him whose feast we celebrate may serve to heal us: through Christ our Lord. Amen.

October 3

S. TERESA OF THE CHILD JESUS

Ant.

THE Lord   *   will always grant thee rest and fill thy soul with brightness; thou shalt be like a well-watered field or a never-failing fountain.

℟ The Lord will be to thee eternal light.

℣ And thy God will be thy glory.

Let us pray: *Prayer*

LORD, who hast said: unless you become like little children, you shall not enter the kingdom of heaven; grant, we pray thee, that by following the blessed maid Teresa in humility and singleness of heart, we may win the prize

of everlasting glory: thou who livest and
reignest for ever and ever.
Amen.

October 15

S. TERESA

Ant.

THE Lord   *   gave her wisdom
and prudence exceeding great, and a
heart wide as the sand on the sea shore.

℟. The Lord helped her with the light
of his countenance.

℣. The Lord is within her and he
shall not desert her.

Let us pray: *Prayer*

LISTEN to us, God our Saviour, so that
we who find joy in the festival of thy
blessed maiden Teresa may be nourished
by her inspired teaching and learn from
her the spirit of godly service: through
Christ our Lord.   Amen.

October 21

S. HILARION

Ant.

WELL done   *   thou good and
faithful servant; because thou hast
been faithful over a few things I will

place thee over many things, saith the Lord.

℞ The just shall spring as the lily.

℣. And flourish for ever before the Lord.

Let us pray: *Prayer*

ALMIGHTY and eternal God, who art always and everywhere admirable in the merits of thy blessed confessor Hilarion, we beseech thy clemency that as thou hast raised him to a high degree of glory, so by the help of his prayers, we may obtain mercy: through Christ our Lord.   Amen.

October 30

S. SERAPION

Ant.

WELL done   *   thou good and faithful servant; because thou hast been faithful over a few things I will place thee over many things, saith the Lord.

℞ The just shall spring as the lily.

℣. And flourish for ever before the Lord.

Let us pray: *Prayer*

O God who hast willed that thy blessed confessor and bishop Serapion should shine in thy Church by his learning and virtue; grant, we pray, that through the merits and prayers of him whose feast we celebrate, we may imitate his zeal in the pursuit of true wisdom and holiness: through Christ our Lord.   Amen.

November 4

BL. FRANCES D'AMBOISE

Ant.

THE kingdom of heaven   *   is like a net that was cast into the sea, and enclosed fish of every kind at once; when it was full, the fishermen drew it out, and sat on the beach, where they stored all that was worth keeping in their vessels, and threw the useless kind away.

℟ God chose and predestined her.

℣ And gave her a place in his tabernacle.

Let us pray: *Prayer*

O merciful God, enlighten the hearts of thy faithful, and through the efficacious prayers of blessed Frances, teach us to despise worldly comfort and to find

our joy always in heavenly consolation:
through Christ our Lord.   Amen.

November 6

BL. NUNO ALVAREZ PEREIRA

Ant.

REJOICE   *   and praise at the
same time for the Lord hath consoled
his people.

℟ The just shall spring as the lily.

℣ And flourish for ever before
the Lord.

Let us pray: *Prayer*

O God, who didst enable blessed Nuno
to fight the good fight and to win
renown for his victory over self and the
world, grant that we, thy servants, may
vanquish the desire of earthly pleasures
and rejoice eternally in the heavenly
fatherland: through Christ our Lord.
Amen.

November 14

FEAST OF ALL CARMELITE SAINTS

Ant.

THEY went about   *   in sheep
skins and goatskins, destitute, dis-
tressed, afflicted, for the world was not

worthy of them; their home was the desert, the mountain and the cave, but their faith gained them holiness and they received the reward.

℞ God is wonderful in his saints.

℣ And glorious in his majesty.

Let us pray: *Prayer*

ALMIGHTY and merciful God, who makest us rejoice on the annual commemoration of all the saints of the Order of the most blessed Virgin Mary of Mount Carmel: mercifully grant that by their example and merits we may live for thee alone in continual meditation of thy law and with perfect self-abnegation, and with them merit to attain to the happiness of eternal life: through Christ our Lord. Amen.

November 15

COMMEMORATION OF ALL THE DECEASED OF THE ORDER

Ant.

I AM　　*　　the resurrection and the life; he that believeth in me, shall not die for ever.

(No versicle)

Let us pray: *Prayer*

O God, creator and redeemer of all the faithful, grant to the souls of our brothers and sisters forgiveness of all their sins. Let our loving entreaties obtain for them the pardon they have always desired: thou who livest and reignest for ever and ever.   Amen.

November 16

BL. LOUIS MORBIOLI

Ant.

WELL done   *   thou good and faithful servant; because thou hast been faithful over a few things I will place thee over many things, saith the Lord.

℞. The just shall spring as the lily.

℣. And flourish for ever before the Lord.

Let us pray: *Prayer*

O God, who has shown to blessed Louis the riches of thy mercy, mercifully grant that as he, by thy aid, broke the snares of his vices, so may we, through his intercession, be freed by thy grace from the bonds of our sins: through Christ our Lord.   Amen.

November 24

S. JOHN OF THE CROSS

Ant.

HE gave him   *   the knowledge of the saints; he adorned and perfected his work.

℞ The just shall spring as the lily.

℣. And flourish for ever before the Lord.

Let us pray: *Prayer*

GOD, who didst endow thy confessor and doctor John with a spirit of utter self-denial and a pre-eminent love of the cross, grant that by constant following of his example we may win eternal glory: through Christ our Lord.   Amen.

An Act of Consecration to our Lady of Mt. Carmel

O Mary, Queen and Mother of Carmel, I come today to consecrate myself entirely to thee. To thee as the Mother of grace I owe all that I am and all that I have, and my whole life is a small return for the many graces and blessings that have come from God to me through thy hands. Since thou regardest with an eye of special kindness those who wear thy scapular, I implore thee to strengthen my weakness with thy power, to enlighten the darkness of my mind with thy wisdom, to increase in me faith, hope and charity that I may render, day by day, my debt of humble homage to thee.

May thy scapular keep thine eyes of mercy turned towards me and bring me thy special protection in the daily struggle to be faithful to thy Divine Son and to thee. May it separate me from all that is sinful in life and remind me constantly of my duty to behold thee and to clothe myself with thy virtues. From henceforth I shall strive to live in the sweet companionship of thy spirit, to offer all to Jesus through thee and to make my life the mirror of thy humility, charity, patience, meekness and prayerfulness.

O dearest Mother, support me by thy never-failing love so that I, an unworthy sinner, may come one day to exchange thy scapular for the wedding garment of heaven and dwell with thee and the saints of Carmel in the kingdom of thy Son.

Amen.

Indulgence: 300 days each time: plenary indulgence if recited daily for a whole month under the usual conditions for gaining a plenary indulgence.